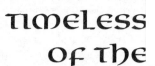

TIMELESS
OF THE

 a beginner's guide

STEVE EDDY AND CLAIRE HAMILTON

Hodder & Stoughton

A MEMBER OF THE HODDER HEADLINE GROUP

Acknowledgements

The authors would like to thank Caitlín and John Matthews for permission to quote from their works. The extract from Ammianus Marcellinus is reprinted by permission of the publishers and the Loeb Classical Library from *Ammianus Marcellinus Vol. I*, translated by John C. Rolfe, Cambridge, Mass.: Harvard University Press, 1935, revised 1950.

The authors and publisher would like to thank Oxford University Press for permission to reproduce the poem on page 82, Anon – from *Medieval Irish Lyrics*, James Carney (Dublin, 1967) reprinted in *The New Oxford Book of Irish Verse*, edited by Thomas Kinsella, 1986, and the poem on page 83, Anon – from *A Golden Treasury of Irish Poetry*, David Greene and Frank O'Connor (eds) (London, 1967) reprinted in *The New Oxford Book of Irish Verse*, edited by Thomas Kinsella, 1986.

Every effort has been made to contact the holders of copyright material but if any have been inadvertently overlooked, the publisher will be pleased to make the necessary alterations at the first opportunity.

ISBN 0 340 74285 2

First published 1999
Impression number   10 9 8 7 6 5 4 3 2 1
Year   2003 2002 2001 2000 1999

Typeset by Transet Ltd, Coventry, England.
Printed in Great Britain for Hodder & Stoughton Educational,
a division of Hodder Headline Plc, 338 Euston Road, London NW1 3BH
by Cox & Wyman Limited, Reading, Berks.

Contents

Chapter 1   Who were the Celts?... 1

Archaeological evidence 2

Classical references.. 4

Mythical sources 6

Irish myths 6

Welsh myths 7

The Book of Invasions..................................... 7

Chapter 2   The sacred land 8

The Four Elements.. 9

Life, death and legend..................................... 12

The Elemental Pledge 13

The Four Directions... 13

The Five Provinces of Ireland 13

The Four Elements and the Magical Objects . 14

The sense of place 15

Chapter 3   Goddesses and gods 18

The land.. 19

Totem animals 20

The Goddess 20

Dark goddesses 21

Horse goddesses.. 22

The Bright Goddess 23

Celtic gods 23

The old gods 24

The New God... 25

The Young Son.. 25

Eloquence 26

The Sea God.. 26

Welsh deities.. 26

The cult of the head... 27

Chapter 4   The hero... 29

Celtic courage 29

The character of the hero 31

Geasa... 32

Curses 33

Cu Chulainn – a model hero........................... 34

Chapter 5   Appearance and reality 38

Shape-shifting... 40

The tale of Blodeuwedd, the flower bride...... 40

Taliesin 42

Chapter 6 The wheel of the year 45

A lunar calendar 46

The Celtic festivals 47

Solar festivals 50

Celtic astrology and tree calendars 50

Chapter 7 The Otherworld.. 52

Under earth, over sea 53

Love between the worlds 54

Animus, anima and soul loss............................. 56

The Celts and reincarnation............................. 57

Chapter 8 The Druids 59

Bards 60

Ovates 62

The Ogham alphabet... 62

Druids 64

Brehons 64

Beliefs... 65

Ritual.. 65

Sacrifices... 66

The fall of the Druids....................................... 67

Chapter 9 Truth, honour and justice 70

The power of naming.. 71

The poet's power 71

Honour 73

Justice... 74

The position of women 76

Chapter 10 The Celtic Church.. 78

Pagan to Christian 79

St Columba 80

The Christianizing of myth 81

Loricas.. 83

Celtic Christianity *versus* Rome...................... 83

Pelagianism... 84

Conclusion 87

Bibliography and discography... 89

Index 91

Chapter 1

Who were the Celts?

The Celts were considered by the ancient Greeks and Romans to be barbarians. Yet the Greeks, as far back as 500 BCE, called them Keltoi – the root word of which means 'Hero', but which also carries with it the sense of 'Strangers' or 'Mysterious ones'. Certainly there was something strange and different about the Celts, something alien that the classical world could not penetrate or understand, yet which it found fascinating. Down the centuries the Celts have kept their reputation as a secret people, guardians of an unknown lore. What was so different and mysterious about the Celts and why is it that we are now nearer than ever to understanding the secret life of the Celtic people? This book seeks to find answers to these questions and in so doing to uncover some of the ancient mysteries as well as showing their relevance to contemporary thinking, and how they could be vital to modern-day living.

It is difficult to penetrate the Celtic mysteries because the Celts guarded their way of life and their beliefs. They did not believe in writing anything down, yet they greatly honoured their history and culture, and therefore maintained strict schools of instruction for memorizing all these facts. In this way they raised the oral tradition to heights never attempted before or since. They also had great veneration for those who kept their history alive in this way. These were the Druids, the priestly caste who would, typically, spend twenty years memorizing the Celtic heritage in verse and telling it to the accompaniment of a small harp-like instrument at great feasts.

Because the Celts were unable or unwilling to write anything about themselves, we are dependent on outside sources of knowledge about them. There are three main sources available to us. Firstly, we have archaeological evidence from the uncovering of Celtic burial sites; secondly, we have some descriptions of them given by classical writers; and thirdly, some of the old tales of gods and heroes, handed down orally at the time, were eventually written down by Christian monks as a historical record of these peoples. The combined evidence from these sources suggests that far from being a barbaric people, the Celts could boast a highly developed and complex culture rich in myth, philosophical and spiritual learning, religious practice and artistic genius, not to mention their technical proficiency and their great valour and prowess in warfare.

Archaeological evidence

Excitingly, much of the archaeological evidence dates from the nineteenth century, so it is a comparatively recent source of knowledge. In 1846 an immense prehistoric cemetery was discovered just above Hallstatt village near Salzburg in Austria, containing about two and a half thousand graves dated between 700 and 500 BCE. This major discovery relates to the earliest fully Celtic peoples. Previously there had been the Urnfield peoples, the proto-Celts of the Bronze Age. The Hallstatt period relates to the Iron Age. Among the findings were four-wheel chariots, horse-harnesses, finely decorated vessels and iron swords patterned with gold-leaf, ivory and amber. There was evidence of extensive trade in, for example, Phoenician glass and amber from the Baltic.

The second and more refined phase of Celtic evolution can be dated by a further rich discovery made in 1858 after a drought lowering a lake near La Tène in Switzerland brought to light another site. This dates from 500 BCE and contained more finely wrought and sophisticated artefacts, among them numerous amphorae and other vessels for mixing and containing wine, bronze flagons and cups, as well as jewellery and weapons showing extensive use of distinctively flowing Celtic patterns, sometimes using classical and even Eastern motifs.

From such evidence it has been deduced that the earliest Celts were located in central Europe between the rivers Elbe, Danube and Rhine. They spread out over the next few centuries across mid-Europe, Gaul, Spain and the British Isles. In early times they were friendly with the Greeks and were allied with them against the Phoenicians and the Persians. Around 500 BCE the Celts took Spain from the Carthaginians and, a hundred years later, northern Italy from the Etruscans. At this time, they were also on good terms with the Romans and had allied with them against the Carthaginians. However, the Romans played them false and the Celts, after seeking satisfaction from Rome and finding none, took revenge by sacking Rome in 390 BCE. In 300 BCE they settled in Cisalpine Gaul, but after this time, their power began to decline. At the best of times they had been a people made up of a collection of tribes. They had been extraordinarily unified through custom and belief, but now they began to split up again.

This Celtic bronze tendril is reminiscent of Paisley pattern, suggesting Celtic Indo-European origins, or the influence of trade with the Middle East

Taking the law into their own hands, one tribe went to northern Greece and sacked the shrine at Delphi in 273 BCE; others continued the struggle with Rome, only to be massacred in two great battles. Finally the previously subjugated Germanic tribes rose up against the Celts, who retreated to their final strongholds in Gaul and the British Isles. By the time Christianity had taken hold, the Celts had been conquered by the Romans and had nowhere to escape except for the far west of Britain – Wales, Cornwall and Ireland. Nevertheless at their period of greatest expansion the Celtic world extended, amazingly, from Ireland and part of Spain in the west to Hungary and Czechoslovakia in the east and from northern Scotland down to northern Italy and former Yugoslavia.

The Celts were divided into two main language groups, known as Brythonic or P-Celtic and Goidelic or Q-Celtic. The Brythonic group survives in the languages of Wales, Brittany and Cornwall, the Goidelic in the Gaelic languages of Scotland, Ireland and the Isle of Man. The P-Celtic term derives from the Brythonic habit of replacing all *k*, *q* or *c* sounds with *p*. For example, the Gaelic *mac* (son of) becomes *map* or *ap*.

Classical references

The first observer of the Celts was appreciative of them. Helicanos of Lesbos in the fifth century BCE described them as valuing justice and righteousness. Another Greek philosopher, Posidonius, of the Stoic school in the first century BCE, also commented on the Celtic peoples. Unfortunately his writings are lost but his observations reappear in those of later historians. These include Caesar, then Strabo, Diodorus Siculus and Lucan, who all wrote around the first century CE, then Dio Cassius at the end of the second century CE. Taken together these writers provide substantial material on the Celts. However, they tend to concentrate on their more outlandish and 'Barbarian' customs such as ritual practices, divination, human sacrifice and head-hunting. No proper picture emerges of the Celtic gods and goddesses, or of the religious system which other evidence suggests was their strongest and most civilized characteristic. Also, of course, they received a bad press after sacking Rome and

Delphi. Plato, for example, describes them in his *Laws* as 'drunken and combative'.

It is, therefore, very important to be aware of the prejudices of those writing about the Celts. Because their temperament was passionate and spontaneous, it was often at odds with classical logicality. As Polybius observed: 'I say not usually, but always, in everything they attempt, they are driven headlong by their passions and never submit to the laws of reason.' Thus to the over-disciplined and rational Romans the Celts seemed lawless and undisciplined. Many writers, however, noted their highly cultivated use of language. Because the Celts forbade the use of written words, the power of the spoken word was very important to them, though even here they employed a certain secrecy. They believed that eloquence was more powerful than force of arms. Yet they were known for their love of war. Strabo called them 'war-mad' (4.4.1–2), while Cato reflected that their love of eloquence was at least as strong as their love of war.

As to their way of life, Strabo describes the Gaulish Celts in his *Geography* (4.4.3):

> *Most of them, even to the present time, sleep on the ground, and eat their meals seated on beds of straw. Food they have in very great quantities, along with milk and flesh of all sorts, but particularly the flesh of hogs, both fresh and salted … As for their houses, which are large and dome-shaped, they make them of planks and wicker, throwing over them quantities of thatch.*

Ammianus Marcellinus says the Gauls 'with equal care keep clean and neat, and in those districts, particularly in Aquitania, no man or woman can be seen, be she never so poor in soiled and ragged clothing' (15.12.1–2). Strabo also comments on the strictness of their attention to their figures: 'any young man who exceeds the standard measure of the girdle is punished' (4.4.6).

Diodorus comments on how they highlight their blonde hair with lime-water and wear it tied at the back of the head from where it falls down the back of their neck like a horse's mane. According to Herodian the Celts were 'not used to clothes', wearing iron ornaments and tattoos instead.

The concept of the Mother was central to early Celtic society which was matrilinear, and even later on Celtic society maintained a degree of matriarchy, a fact which the Romans found offensive. Strabo, for example, considered it a mark of barbarism that Celtic women enjoyed more power than their Roman counterparts. For example, Celtic women were able to lead armies, to follow professions, to become Druids, to inherit property and to initiate divorce.

Mythical sources

The purpose of myth is to record the past, to entertain, to instruct and to inspire. For the Celts it was also a way of creating a framework of belief on which they could base their conduct. Of the three branches of Celtic mythology – Irish, Welsh and Gaulish – only Irish and Welsh survive because they were recorded by the early Christian monks. Such manuscripts, although sometimes fragmentary and obviously Christianized in places, offer perhaps the most exciting key to understanding Celtic thinking. They are peopled with larger-than-life characters, gods and heroic figures who move in a highly imaginative archaic world which conforms to a belief system that is foreign to us but is based on profound philosophies which, if respected, can offer new perspectives and insights for our time.

Although the monks started recording myths as early as the sixth century, the majority of surviving manuscripts date from the twelfth century, but of course the material contained in them is from a much earlier oral tradition.

Irish myths

There are three main cycles: the Mythological Cycle, which includes the *Book of Invasions* (*Leabhar Gabhala*) and the *History of Places* (*Dindsenchas*); the Ulster Cycle, which includes the famous *Cattle Raid of Cooley* (*Tain Bo Cuailnge*); and the Fionn Cycle, which deals with the heroic exploits of Fionn mac Cumhail (pronounced 'Fyun macool') and the Fianna, or warrior band. All these were compiled in the twelfth century but the *Tain* is also contained in one of the oldest manuscripts, *The Book of the Dun Cow*, so-called because it was apparently based on a manuscript written by St Ciaran in the seventh century on the hide of his favourite cow.

Welsh myths

These are not so extensive as their Irish counterparts, and were written down much later. Nevertheless, many of the stories contain elements from the old oral tradition. The earliest surviving collections are found in *The White Book of Rhydderch* (c.1300) and *The Red Book of Hergest* (c. 1500). These manuscripts contain the important tales of the *Mabinogion*. The *Mabinogion* proper contains four main branches or tales concerning Pwyll, Branwen, Manawydan and Math. There are also seven other stories, of which three are early Arthurian tales. In Lady Charlotte Guest's translation she includes a twelfth story, that of Taliesin, which comes from a later source.

The Book of Invasions

This mythical history of Ireland was compiled by the monks. It is recounted by a Druidic figure named Tuan who lives through the successive generations, changing into various animals (see Chapter 5). In his account the most influential race, the Tuatha de Danann, or Children of the goddess Danu, had to defend Ireland from the Fomorians, a race of giants who had demonic characteristics. They also had to fight the Firbolgs, or 'men of the bags' who were believed to have come from Southern Europe. They waged the two great battles of Moytura against these races and finally drove them out. The Tuatha claimed to have come from four great cities – Falias, Gorias, Finias and Murias, in which they had been taught by sages and from which they brought magical treasures. These were respectively the Stone of Destiny, the Sword of Lugh, the Magic Spear and the Cauldron of the Dagda. The Tuatha were arguably the gods of Ireland who eventually had to capitulate to the Milesians, or human race. However, a compromise was reached in which they were allowed to remain in the burial mounds or *sidhe* where they exist to this day as the fairy people.

Chapter 2
The sacred land

It is hard for us to imagine what a truly Celtic consciousness would be like. However, the evidence suggests that to the Celts all things were sacred, but that some things were more sacred than others. We can see from the same sources that the Celts had a reverence for nature – one that we could learn from. They lived amongst it and their yearly cycle of festivals reflected their dependence on it. They saw nature, however, as 'the land', which in turn embodied the Great Mother in all her guises. Within the land, specific local sites were seen as manifestations of a whole pantheon of deities.

To the pagan Irish, the High King was wedded to the land. This was ritually observed in a ceremony in which he had intercourse with a white mare (representing the goddess of the land) and then drank a broth made with her flesh. The human queen to whom the king was husband in the more conventional sense was seen as an embodiment of the Goddess, linked with earth goddesses, such as Macha and Brigid. There were also great queens who ruled in their own right, such as Medb (pronounced 'Maeve'), Cartimandua and Boudicca, who were also associated with the Goddess. We are reminded of the land-goddess link when the hero Cu Chulainn (pronounced 'Cuhulan'), the Hound of Ulster, woos his intended bride with riddles, gazing at her bosom and declaring, 'That is a fair land. How I wish I could wander there.'

The Four Elements

The Celtic view of nature takes on a new sophistication when we consider the role of the Four Elements in Celtic cosmology. To the Celts, the universe was made up of four forces, manifesting as earth, air, fire and water. This belief was widespread, and probably first formalized by Aristotle, but the Celts almost certainly developed it independently. These four forces provide a focus for worship and ritual, and play a key part in myth and legend. We will now look at the associations of each element.

Earth

Earth is the realm of the Great Mother. The Underworld is beneath the earth and one way to reach it is through cave entrances. One such entrance was at the Cave of Cruachan, near the court of Queen Medb in Connacht. Another entrance is said to exist on Glastonbury Tor. In Irish tales, too, the Otherworld (see page 53) is sometimes reached through the *sidhe*, the earth mounds of the *Tuatha de Danann*. Also in Ireland, the burial sites of Newgrange and Tara, pre-Celtic in origin but revered by the Celts, were regarded as gates to the Otherworld.

Thus earth is associated with death – but then death, to the Celts, is a necessary precursor of life and fertility. The element of earth can also be associated with material reality, solidity, practicality and limitations – with which we all need to be in touch if we are to avoid being 'away with the fairies'.

Air

Air, in nature, is represented by the sky, and by winds and storms. According to Roman writers, there were Celtic sky gods, and some Celtic rituals involved the constellations, especially the Pleiades. The Druids worshipped in sacred groves, perhaps because trees form a link between earth and sky. Mistletoe, an important plant in Druidic ritual and medicine, is associated with the sun and, therefore with fire, but also with air, since it never touches the ground and, therefore, appears to be a gift of the gods from out of the sky. Birds, as creatures of the air, play a special part in divination, and the Druids were said to have mastered the art of magical flight.

The element of air relates to freedom of movement, intellect and communication. Whereas earth gives form, air is the space that defines form, as well as the coming and going of ideas.

Fire

The principle of fire is found in any source of heat, but its ultimate source is the sun. Some Celtic gods have solar associations, especially Mabon, the Son of Light (later associated with Christ, crucified on the Cross of the Elements). In its physical form fire keeps wild animals at bay, and draws people together. It also converts matter into energy – and raw meat into a meal! It appears in many Celtic cleansing rituals, and notably at the festival of Beltain. The element of fire is associated with energy, dynamism, action and enthusiasm. Without it, we would achieve nothing.

Water

The element of water was particularly important to the Celts, who saw every spring, stream, river and lake as the expression of a particular deity. The River Severn, for example, was the outward form of the goddess Sabrann, or Sabrina. Sulis was the dark goddess who presided over the sacred thermal spring at what was to become Aquae Sulis – Bath. Manannan and Dylan were both gods of the sea.

Examples of how water gateways were used in ritual include the circling of a well three times in a clockwise direction (deosil), in order to evoke its powers. When Boann tested the well of wisdom at the source of the Boyne by circling it three times anticlockwise (widdershins) the river boiled up and attacked her. According to a slightly different version of the story, Boann was turned into a river by her husband Nechtan for releasing its waters to the people of Ireland.

In Brittany, where the Church made special efforts to graft itself on to the native paganism, many pre-Christian holy wells were officially sanctified by the severed head of a deceased saint. Even in modern-day Ireland, there are hundreds of 'holy wells' where offerings are left – an echo of pagan belief. In Jordan Hill, Dorset, strange offerings were found in a dry well: cists containing ironwork and sixteen pairs of tiles, each pair containing a coin and the body of a crow.

Votive offerings have been found in great numbers at several lake, river and bog sites. At Llyn Cerrig Bach, on Anglesey, there were offerings of cauldrons, weapons and chariots, deposited from the second century BCE to the first century CE. Another Welsh lake site, Llyn Fawr in Mid Glamorgan, produced cauldrons probably sunk there around 600 BCE. Similar findings have been made at La Tène, on Lake Neuchatel in Switzerland, dated to around 100 BCE. Animal remains were also found at this site.

The Thames must have been associated with a war or smith god, as many weapons have been found in it. At the same time, rivers and springs have been associated with healing, especially for the Romano–Celts, who brought wooden models of their diseased or injured body parts to the shrine, in the hope of getting healthy ones back.

Bogs and marshes were perhaps particularly sacred, as they combined land with water, and since they were potentially dangerous places, perhaps the dwelling places of spirits who needed to be propitiated. The famous Gundestrup cauldron was found in a bog.

A warrior being dipped in a cauldron, shown on the Gundestrup cauldron

This combination of land and water is also found where land meets water, especially the seashore, the Celtic place of poetic inspiration. Water is associated with emotion, artistic inspiration, dreams and the unconscious – all part of the traditionally 'feminine', right-brain area without which our vitality dries up. However, for inspiration to find expression, the form-giving quality of earth is required.

Life, death and legend

The elements feature strongly in Celtic ritual. Fire was carried around infants, houses and fields in the solar direction to protect them with the sun's power. There was also an Irish Druidic baptism, called *baisteadh geinntlidhe*, 'the rain wedge of protection'. More gruesomely, the Druids occasionally practised human sacrifice, usually as a form of divination. This could be by live burial (earth), drowning (water), hanging (air), or burning in a 'wicker man' (fire). The body of one victim, a young man, was found preserved in a bog at Lindow Moss. He had been stunned, garrotted, bled and then thrown into the water naked.

Celtic tradition suggests that we must be elementally balanced in order to live. One story relating to this is of the king who tried to test a Druid's powers by bringing him a boy and asking the Druid how he would die. The king presented the boy in three disguises, each time asking the same question. Each time the Druid predicted death by a different element – to the king's amusement. However, the boy grew to be a man, and was thrown from his horse over a cliff (earth), into a tree, where he was caught dangling by one foot (air), with his head in a river (water).

The elements also appear in legend. In the tale of the Welsh poet Taliesin (see Chapter 5), Ceridwen pursues Gwion Bach through four magical transformations:

Gwion	Ceridwen	Element
hare	greyhound	earth
fish	otter	water
bird	falcon	air
corn	hen	fire

As a grain of corn (ripened by the sun – fire), Gwion is gobbled up by Ceridwen-as-hen, as a result of which she eventually gives birth to the poet Taliesin: the circle of the elements therefore leads to creativity.

The Elemental Pledge

If I break faith with you, may the skies fall upon me, may the seas drown me, may the earth rise up and swallow me.

The Four Directions

Closely linked to the Four Elements are the Four Directions, or *Airts* (see diagram). This symbolic use of the compass points is similar to that of Native American shamanism and Chinese *Feng Shuei*. These were important in Celtic ritual and magic. Each direction is linked to an element: north–earth; south–fire; west–water; east–air.

If we are meditating on the qualities of a particular element we will find it helpful to face in the appropriate direction.

The Five Provinces of Ireland

The land of Ireland, as it was at one time divided, is a physical manifestation of the spiritual principles of the Four Directions. It consisted of four provinces, with a fifth central province, Meath, symbolically uniting them under one sacred rule. In addition, each of the four outer provinces was associated with a magical object, or gift, and with a quality:

Direction	Element	Province	Object	Quality
North	Earth	Ulster	Stone	War
West	Water	Connacht	Cauldron	Knowledge
East	Air	Leinster	Sword	Prosperity
South	Fire	Munster	Spear	Music
Centre	Ether	Meath	Throne	Sovereignty

This could be seen as forming the mythical-ideological basis for the unity of Ireland – in relation to which it is interesting to note the quality associated with Ulster.

The Four Elements and the Magical Objects

According to the mythical history of Ireland, the Tuatha de Danann arrived bearing four magical possessions: the Stone of Destiny, the Spear of Lugh, the Sword of Nuada and the Cauldron of the Dagda. Each was identified with an element.

The Stone of Destiny

Earth being one with the land, and kings being wedded to the land, it is not surprising to find that the High Kings of Ireland were crowned standing on the Lia Fail, or Stone of Destiny. It was said to roar when the rightful monarch stood on it. According to some, this stone is the Stone of Scoon, now in Westminster Abbey; others identify it as a stone standing upright on the Hill of Tara, in Meath. Stones were used generally for the swearing of oaths; it was thought that the ancestors, who lived under the earth, bore witness.

The great stone circles were probably used for Druidic rituals and were believed to contain powerful earth energies. The cult of the stone was, therefore, a very ancient one, and it lasted into Christian times. The Romano-Celtic stone altars evolved into Christian altars, and the great high crosses with their elaborate carvings became a particular feature of the Celtic Church. Even today dolmens with holes in them, as well as pierced stones, are considered special. The custom of passing sick children through the hole, with its connotation of rebirth, still persists and with it the remnant of an understanding of the healing power of the land.

The Spear of Lugh

The spear is identified with fire. Because of its association with the sun, fire is linked to the cult of the hero. The spear, in turn, represents the hero's single-pointed aim and direct action. The god Lugh was associated with crafts and one can see a connection between this kind of directed action and the craftsman's applied inspiration. Smiths, who worked with fire, were considered to have magical powers. The goddess Brigid was also associated with crafts, and the Celts kept a sacred fire burning for her.

The Sword of Nuada

When the Tuatha de Danann came to Ireland they used their arts to disguise themselves in the element of air – arriving like a mist over the water. The sword is a symbol of truth. Instead of swords the Druids carried wands made from trees, particularly hazel which denoted wisdom. Air corresponds to the power of the mind, and to the breath of life. Perfume and music are also related to air. The Druids used wands hung with bronze, silver or gold bells, together with incense, to summon Otherworldly spirits.

The Cauldron of the Dagda

The Cauldron is associated with water, and therefore with the feminine. Many Celtic cauldrons have been unearthed by archaeologists. The most spectacular is the Gundestrup cauldron, found in Denmark. This depicts the god Cernunnos surrounded by animals on one panel, and a string of warriors, one of whom appears to be being dipped into a cauldron (see page 11). The Dagda's cauldron produced limitless supplies of food, as well as reviving dead warriors. The cauldron, therefore, appears to have been a symbol of rebirth.

The sense of place

The Celts believed that a place was forever imprinted with the events that had taken place there. Thus Druids were able to learn a place's history by divinatory means (see Chapter 8). This belief is not limited to the Celts. For example, Rudolf Steiner wrote about the 'akashic records' in a similar vein, and most of us have associations with places where important events – personal or historic – have taken place. The practice of tuning in to the vibrations of past events present in a place is called 'psychometry'.

An expression of this belief was in the importance ascribed to naming a place. A name would reflect a quality – often a spiritual quality, associated with a god, or an event, and the name would carry power. *The White Book of Rhydderch* lists the names of Britain, including 'Island of Honey'. The Irish place-name stories, the *Dindsenchas*, give explanations of place-names throughout the land, some rather artificial, but others preserving true traditions. When Cu Chulainn, whose wooing of Emer is touched on earlier, recounts the route by which he has reached his bride to be, he replies in the poetic language of the *Dindsenchas*:

> *From the Cover of the Sea, over the Great Secret of the Tuatha de Danaan, and the Foam of the two steeds of Emain Macha; over the Morrigu's Garden, and the Great Sow's Back; over the Glen of the Great Dam, between god and his prophet …*

trans. C. Matthews

Naturally she understands him.

Given the power of Celtic place-names, it is interesting that while only a handful of Celtic words have survived into ordinary modern-day English ('brock', a badger, is one; 'pony' may come from the Celtic horse goddess Epona), many place-names are Celtic. Though some are settlement names, such as Billingsgate, London (from the god Bel), the vast majority are river names: Avon, Dee, Derwent, Dart, Don, Esk, Axe, Exe, Ouse, Severn, Tees, Thames, Trent and Wye are all Celtic. Perhaps the power of the water deities awed the Saxons sufficiently for them to preserve the names.

Application

Experiencing the elements

The first step towards developing a sense of place is to focus on each element in turn. Aim to envelop yourself in the essence of the element. Go to a place where you can experience the elements. Observe them and allow your mind to cast up associations with each element. As you watch the wind move the trees and feel it on your skin, you may think of 'the winds of change', or what is carried on the wind – leaves, messages, communications. The heat of the sun may fill you with a sense of well-being, while a flickering flame may suggest energy and inspiration. Running water will tend to soothe, suggesting the waters of life, running on forever, but always changing.

Absorb the energy of each element, and then of the particular place. You may find it helpful to go back repeatedly to the same place for quiet meditation. It will then become your special place, where you easily feel at one with yourself and nature. If you cannot go out into a safe and secluded natural place, you can conjure one up from memory or imagination, taking time to build up your inner impressions.

Chapter 3

Goddesses and gods

In *The Conquest of Gaul* Caesar gives a report of the Celtic gods in which he tries to press them into the Roman mould. However, there is evidence to show that the Celtic idea of religion was very different from that of the Romans. Whereas the Romans gave their gods definite names and attributes and made statues and likenesses of them, the Celts conceived of their gods in much vaguer and more generalized terms.

Just as the Celts preferred not to fix words in written form, they were relatively reluctant to fashion fixed images of their gods, to give them readily identifiable attributes, or even to name them. Moreover, they believed in the power of name and did not want enemies to know the names of their gods. Thus a common Celtic oath was 'I swear by the gods of my people'. But, more significantly perhaps, the Celts' concept of deity was paradoxically both more mysterious and more immediate than that of other people's. It was also more integrated with everyday life.

In *Man and his Symbols* Jung says: 'What psychologists call psychic identity, or "mystical participation" has been stripped off our world of things.' For the Celts, as for many primitive societies today, there was only a thin boundary between this world and the spiritual. A man might go in and out of the spiritual world and participate in it quite freely. The land was peopled with deities; the legends were tales of their powers. Dreams were taken seriously and the filid, or seers, would even have communal dreams on behalf of the tribe, surrounded and aided by 'Awen' or watchers.

By partaking in ritual and believing in a world of cosmic forces, the Celts gave themselves a world-view and a context in which to conduct their lives. They respected the autonomy of their gods and did not attempt to systemize them. This seems to have been one of the main differences between the Celtic and Roman approach to godhead, and is indicative of the very different outlooks of the two peoples. By not labelling their gods they left them untamed. In their art they preferred pattern, riddle and allusion to representation. Archaeological evidence in the form of depictions, inscriptions and statues is therefore mostly a feature of Romano-Celtic times.

The land

Celtic deities were essentially connected to the land. The power of place was fundamental. The Goddess or Great Mother was identified with the land itself. It was she who was held in the greatest reverence. What seems to emerge from Celtic belief is the interconnectedness of the power of the goddesses and gods with the land and with mortals.

Although there were deities connected with rivers, springs, hills and caves, Celtic belief was more than simple animism. It formed a model for understanding life based on the theory that the health of the tribe depended upon the health of the land. The land was considered sacred and worship therefore took place mostly in nature, in certain sacred groves or beside lakes.

There was an emphasis on chthonic gods and in particular the Tuatha de Danann. Neolithic sites of barrows and chambered tombs were considered places of veneration. Caves, fountains, wells and springs were regarded as gateways to the Underworld. This was not a place of punishment but rather a primal realm containing an old wisdom and peopled with important deities. It was also the place of ancestral burial. Mythically it had strong links with the Otherworld.

Totem animals

It was natural for the Celts to include animals in their world-view. But again, it was not a question of simple animal worship, but rather a recognition of their attributes on a symbolic level. They were often associated with individual deities who represented a superior form of the animal's characteristics. Typical totem animals include the boar, the stag, the hawk, the horse, the wolf and the serpent. The boar was considered to have links with the Otherworld and boar meat was placed in the graves of warriors. The serpent also had strong magical links with the Otherworld.

The Goddess

The matriarchal nature of Celtic society sprang from a veneration of the land. The mother goddess ruled and took kings and heroes as her consorts. If they were wounded or disfigured in any way then the health of the land suffered. Early depictions of mother goddess figures have been found but they are usually represented as triple figures.

The triple aspects of the goddess are traditionally those of maiden, mother and crone, but triple-aspecting could also be a means of combining several attributes – again accentuating the more generalized nature of Celtic deities. In Ireland the great goddess Eriu was the embodiment of the land and became the central presence in its poetry and mythology. She was triple-aspected, her other names being Fodla and Banbha. Sometimes the triple motif was itself triplicated, as in the ninefold goddesses on the sacred Isle de Seine who were said to receive the souls of the dead.

The idea of triplicity seems to have been central to Celtic philosophy generally, as shown by the many variations on the 'triskell' motif in Celtic art (see page 21). It could be related to the Hindu belief that all things come into being, become consolidated and then pass away, and to astrology's designation of zodiacal signs in a cycle of cardinal, fixed and mutable.

Triskell terminal of Clevedon torc

Nearly all the pantheon of Irish gods come from the Tuatha de Danann, the children of the goddess Danu or Anu, who is also considered a type of the Great Mother. Welsh Celtic deities come from the *Mabinogion* cycle of myth and are said to be the children of Don. In parts of Britain the mother goddess was simply referred to as Modron – 'mother', and her divine son as Mabon.

Dark goddesses

The concept of the goddess was that of life-giver but in Celtic thinking this was inseparable from sexuality and death. Contrary to later Christian thinking, there was no great division between life and death, light and darkness, good and evil. Rather, life and death, light and dark were seen as dual aspects of the same power. It is no surprise, then, to encounter the fiery red-haired Morrigan, triple-aspected as the goddess of procreation and sexuality, war and death, appearing in Irish myth. This fearsome goddess was triple-aspected with Nemhain and Badhbh, and often shape-changed into a crow or raven with the power to predict unfavourable outcomes in battle. She came from a line of formidable women warriors who schooled the young heroes of the myths in battle lore. Cu Chulainn received martial training from Scathach on the Isle of Skye. Unfortunately she does not seem to have taught him proper respect for war goddesses for, by defying the Morrigan in battle, he brought about his own death. In her destructive aspect the Morrigan resembles such enchantresses as Circe or the Hindu goddess Kali. In the later Arthurian cycle she is linked to Morgan Le Fay.

Ceridwen was the Welsh equivalent of the Morrigan, her two children, one fair and one ugly, symbolizing the light and dark elements of nature. Ceridwen was the keeper of the Cauldron and mistress of shape-shifting. Her totem animal was the boar.

Both these goddesses were a type of the Cailleach, or ancient dark mother, in British and Irish tradition. Her other names include Black Annis or the Hag of Beare. She appears in scraps of ancient legend as being able to change the landscape and control the weather. She, too, guards a cauldron of regeneration. In psychological terms the dark goddess is the dark side of the mother who opposes the hero-son and in so doing paradoxically enables him to achieve his own wisdom and maturity.

Horse goddesses

Interestingly Cu Chulainn is said to have died at the same time as his mare, who tried to defend him by throwing herself on eight of his attackers and also cried tears of blood for him. The link between the Goddess and the King centred on a ritual involving a mare. Horses were very important to the Celts and the horse goddess Epona seems to have been a powerful deity. She is depicted in Celtic inscriptions from Gaul and rides a mare, symbol of fertility. She is also sometimes shown with other symbols of fertility such as fruit or corn. She is possibly linked with the Welsh goddess Rhiannon who, for allegedly murdering her son, was made to act as a horse and carry visitors on her back. It is possible that this tale reflects a time of persecution for the horse cult. A very old mother goddess of the Irish, Macha was also strongly associated with horses. In a legend from the Ulster cycle, while pregnant she was made to race against the king's horses at Emain Macha, the ancient capital of Ulster. She died in childbirth, cursing the men of Ulster so that they would succumb to the pains of childbirth for five days and four nights at times of greatest danger.

The Bright Goddess

The greatest and most enduring of the Irish female deities was Brigid. Said to be the daughter of the Dagda and, as such, perhaps synonymous with Danu, she became revered in Ireland as patroness of poetry. She was triple-aspected, also having attributes of healing and smith-craft. A benign goddess, primarily associated with fire and the hearth, it was said that she hung her cloak on the rays of the sun. Her feast day was 1 February, Imbolc, the pagan spring festival, which later became associated with Candlemas. She is also linked with the Roman goddess Minerva. She later became Christianized and was said to be the Abbess of a monastery in Kildare where, according to Geraldus Cambrensus, a perpetual fire was kept burning, tended by nineteen nuns. As she became Christianized, slowly the aspect of fire became subsumed into that of light. St Brigid or St Bride was also traditionally considered to have been the foster-mother of Christ and also Mary's midwife and to have blessed the Christchild with three drops of pure spring-water. Because of this she is also connected with wells and springs.

Celtic gods

Whereas the female deities were all versions of the great mother goddess, the early male Celtic deities were all tribal. However, by the time of the Roman occupation, Caesar speaks of a more generalized male deity: 'The Gauls affirm that they are all descended from Dis, a common father, and say that this is the tradition of the Druids' (VI.18). The idea of Dis Pater is an intriguing one but there are no inscriptions to him as such. It is thought that this generalized concept is possibly a later development reflecting Roman ideas of patriarchy. But there were also some primal individual gods connected with the underworld who had generalized and far-reaching powers such as Cernunnos and the Dagda.

The old gods

Cernunnos was an ancient and important Celtic god. He survived into Roman times and is found in images from Romano-Celtic sites, though there is only one inscription that bears his name. He was lord of the animals and is usually depicted wearing horns or antlers, the stag being his totem animal. There is a famous image of him on the inside of the Gundestrup cauldron, antlered and sitting cross-legged wearing a torc, with another torc in his right hand and a ram-headed snake in his left. He is surrounded by deer, boar and other wild animals. His image is, therefore, strongly suggestive of shamanistic and shape-changing powers. Cernunnos is also connected with the Underworld and with fertility. It is possible that he later became subsumed into the devil in Christian thinking.

The Dagda was a most important god given great character in Irish myth. He is prominent in the tales concerning the Tuatha de Danann, and was called 'the Good God' – 'good' meaning multi-talented. Although extremely powerful, he was sometimes represented in legend as comical, on occasion wearing a tunic that did not cover his buttocks, and he also carried a huge club which had to be transported on wheels. All this suggests he was connected with an ancient pre-Celtic deity. He was also a great wizard, keeper of a magic harp and of a magic cauldron of abundance which could restore dead warriors to life. He had a huge appetite and was once forced by the Fomorians to eat a huge meal of porridge from his own enormous cauldron, which he did easily. He also had a huge sexual appetite. He is said to have coupled with the Morrigan before the second Battle of Moytura (Magh Tuiredh) while she stood astride the River Unius. He also had an illicit union with Boann (who gave her name to the Boyne) and thereby fathered Aenghus Mac Og, the god of love. This coupling of the gods and goddesses is symbolic of the union of the god with nature. It is notable that the line of succession in Celtic times was matrilinear.

The New God

The Dagda gradually became replaced by Lugh, 'the Bright One'. Lugh was connected with light and the sun. He was guardian of the magic spear of Gorias. Like the Dagda he was multi-skilled and there is an account of his only being admitted to the Fort of Tara on account of his abundance of talents which included carpentry, smithcraft, fighting, harp-playing, storytelling, healing and wizardry. Because of this he took over from Nuada (later called The Silver Hand) as King of the Tuatha de Danann. He helped them to overcome the Fomorians and killed their king, his own grandfather, Balor of the Evil Eye, by a slingshot through the eye. Less-ancient than the Dagda and Cernunnos, he is associated more with the hero of myth. He is said to have been at least the mystical father of Cu Chulainn. His worship was widespread and he became identified with the Roman god Mercury. Caesar claimed that he was worshipped more than all the other Celtic gods. His Welsh counterpart is Lleu from the Fourth Branch of the *Mabinogion*. Lleu is a type of Mabon, the young son, but unlike Lugh is more victim than hero. Lugh also has links with Apollo.

The Young Son

The closest approximation to a Celtic god of love is Angus, the 'Young Son', analogous to the Welsh 'Mabon'. He was a romantic god, associated with youth, beauty, wit and charm. Son of the Dagda and of Boann, the river goddess, he could be said to have been born 'out of time'. This was because the Dagda caused time to appear to stand still for nine months for Boann's husband in order to conceal her illicit pregnancy. By a further trickery concerning time-play Angus managed to obtain lordship of the Bruigh na Boinne (the Boyne Valley) and his palace was said to be at Newgrange. He was a devoted lover of Caer, the Swan Maiden, turning himself into a swan to win her. He also became involved in some famous and fateful love-affairs. He helped Midhir to marry Etain, and Grainne to elope with Diarmid, his foster-son.

Eloquence

Oghma of the honeyed mouth was the god of eloquence. The Celts prized the art of eloquence above that of warfare. The Greek writer Lucian describes a depiction of a figure of Hercules with exquisite thin gold chains running from his tongue to the ears of his followers. This depiction links with Oghma because his Gaulish equivalent, Ogmios, was considered strong and muscular and was associated with Hercules. Oghma is credited with invention of the Ogham alphabet.

The Sea God

Mannanan mac Lir was god of the sea like his father Lir (whose children were famously turned into swans for 900 years by his second wife). His home is traditionally said to be the Isle of Man, which takes his name. He was said to have worn a huge cloak which could change colour. He was master of tricks and illusions and possibly demonstrates the emotional nature of the medium of water. The white-crested waves were known as his horses.

He was also connected to the Otherworld, probably acting as guide to the various magical islands under the sea. His Welsh counterpart would seem to be Manawyddan fab Lyr but he is not connected to the sea. He may, however, have given rise to Shakespeare's King Lear, whose three daughters are strongly suggestive of triple-aspected Celtic goddesses.

Welsh deities

The stories contained in the *Mabinogion* tell of the exploits of heroic figures who are poised somewhere between gods and men. These euhemerized beings are often included in the Celtic pantheon of deities. Thus Arianrhod can be seen as a stellar goddess of the silver wheel and associated with Ariadne, while Blodeuwedd, or 'Flower Maiden', is associated with Persephone. Her transformation into an owl points to the Maiden, Mother and Crone motif. Math the King has godlike powers such as being able to read the thoughts of any of his subjects, and his nephew Gwydion has shape-changing and other magical powers. Lleu Llew Gyffes, his son, is a type of sacrificial king.

The cult of the head

The head had special significance for the Celts, who believed it contained the soul. Warriors cut off the heads of their enemies, replaced the brains with a lime-mixture or preserved the heads with oil and then displayed them as trophies. Numerous carvings of heads were used to decorate doorways and the hallways of ancient sanctuaries. The sacred skull was a feature of the cult of the dead or of the blessed ancestors. Often their skulls were retained and used in rituals at Samhain, the modern Hallowe'en. The head is also venerated in myth. For example in the *Mabinogion* there is the tale of the head of Bran being carried to London by his retinue. The head had magical properties and was able to eat, drink and converse at feast-times. On Bran's orders, and for the purpose of protecting the city, his head was finally buried at the White Mount, which is now the site of the Tower of London. Interestingly the name 'Bran' means 'raven', and there is a saying that if the ravens leave the Tower, the British monarchy will fall.

Application

Visualization

You may like to record this visualization so that you can follow it with your eyes closed. Allow yourself five or ten minutes in which you can relax in a quiet place, free from interruption.

You are standing at the entrance to a stone circle. In front of you the huge stone monoliths form a square gateway into the circle. Take a moment to appreciate your surroundings. When you are ready, step through into the circle. At once you will notice a change in the quality of sound. There is a stillness here. The hum of the busy world is far away. As you remain in the circle, you may become aware of a different kind of humming, increasing in volume. It is the singing of the stones. This is a place of rest but also of power. The stones are connected with the ancient energies of the earth. If you touch some you may find yourself energized; others might drain you of energy. Take what you need from the circle and move on.

You walk for some while now over rolling downland with nothing but the lark between you and the sky for miles around. Now you see ahead of you a wooded valley. You descend into the wood. It is cool and dark after the bright sunlight. Become aware of the myriad life-forms that are here. Use especially your senses of smell, touch, and hearing. You become aware that you are tired and need rest and refreshment. Listen for the sound of a trickling stream and head towards it. The sound is coming from a dense grove of trees. You push your way through and find to your astonishment that you are in a clearing at the centre of which is a fountain in a marble basin with a gold cup lying beside it. You approach the fountain and dip the cup into its pure clear water. This fountain is sacred and belongs to the Goddess. Its waters are the Waters of Life. Drink with reverence and take your time. Imagine that the sounds of the fountain become the tinkling notes of a harp. Imagine, too, the Lady of the Fountain. She has a radiant face of wisdom and beauty. Perhaps you have a question to ask her. When you have drunk your fill you lie down on the marble sill of the fountain and sleep.

You wake up shivering. You are surrounded by the dark forms of trees with the menacing sound of the wind shaking their branches. You get up stiffly. In the distance you can see a red glow. You make your way towards it and discover another clearing deeper in the woods in which a fire is burning. You are fearful of going too near because it is attended by tall figures and animals. As you approach cautiously one of the figures comes towards you. She is veiled and beckons you to come nearer. As you come up close, she lifts her veil and reveals an ancient, wizened face. At first you are taken aback, but something in her eyes holds you. Looking into her eyes you feel as if all the universe is contained in them. You are aware of time's circular path, of the turning of the planets, of the interplay of dark and light, good and evil, knowledge and ignorance, death and regeneration. Stay with her and see what she has to tell you. Perhaps she has the answer to your question. When she dismisses you, leave her courteously and make your way out of the wood, across the downland and back into the stone circle. You may like to stay and meditate a while on what she has told you. When you are ready open your eyes.

Chapter 4

The hero

Most cultures of the ancient world featured the cult of the hero. Joseph L. Henderson, in *Man and his Symbols* (ed. Jung) comments on the widespread similarities:

> *Over and over again one hears a tale describing a hero's miraculous but humble birth, his early proof of superhuman strength, his rapid rise to prominence or power, his triumphant struggle with the forces of evil, his fallibility to the sin of pride … and his fall through betrayal or a 'heroic' sacrifice that ends in his death.*

In Henderson's opinion, heroes are 'symbolic representatives of the whole psyche, the larger and more comprehensive identity that the personal ego lacks'. We could add that they also offer role models, as well as representing a form of propitiatory sacrifice to the gods. Thus they represent both our potential and our earthly limitations: we may achieve greatness, but in the end even the greatest are overcome.

Celtic courage

Celtic legends show a strongly developed form of this hero cult. In addition the Celts as a race were known for their courage. Marcellinus notes that 'the old man marches out on a campaign with a courage equal to that of the man in the prime of life ... and he will make light of many formidable dangers'. (XV.12.3)

Celtic women were equally courageous, as Tacitus confirms when he quotes Boudicca's words to her troops before her final battle with the Romans:

> *We British are used to woman commanders in war. ... I am descended from mighty men! But now I am not fighting for my kingdom and wealth. I am fighting as an ordinary person for my lost freedom, my bruised body, and my outraged daughters. Nowadays Roman rapacity does not even spare our bodies. Old people are killed, virgins raped. But the gods will grant us the vengeance we deserve ... Consider how many of you are fighting – and why. Then you will win this battle, or perish. That is what I, a woman, plan to do! Let the men live in slavery if they will. (XIV.34)*

The Snettisham torc

The Celts, male and female, were known for their recklessly courageous battle charge, which remained their main battle tactic right up to the eighteenth century. Some warriors, the *gaesatae*, even went into battle wearing only a torc around the neck, believing that nakedness conferred magical protection; a gold statuette in the British Museum depicts just such a warrior. Sadly, however, courage and magical protection were not enough. Boudicca – like other Celtic chieftains – was in the end routed by Roman organization and discipline, just as the Highlanders were routed at Culloden by the more calculated military methodology of the English.

The character of the hero

The most obvious characteristic of the Celtic legendary hero is physical courage. A key difference between the ancient Celtic view of courage and our own is that Celtic heroes were fearless, whereas in modern times courage can mean overcoming one's fears – probably a more realistic aim than that of fearlessness. The Celtic hero was also prodigiously strong. However, there was more to Celtic heroism than the ability to kill fifty foes before breakfast without so much as a tremor of anxiety.

The Celtic hero was handsome, intelligent, educated, eloquent and possessed of many accomplishments. The great Irish hero Cu Chulainn (see page 34) is trained in speech and oratory by the poet Sencha, and learns magical arts, including the use of Ogham, from the Druid Amergin (see pages 71–2). He goes to live with the warrior prophetess Scathach in order to learn the arts of war, and also learns the arts of love from her daughter. Similarly the later hero and leader of the Fianna, Fionn mac Cumhail, goes to study poetry with the Druid Finegas, and acquires the gifts of clairvoyance and prophecy when he eats the Salmon of Knowledge.

Despite the battle fury that is often an essential part of the Celtic hero's strength, he is also characterized by presence of mind. One of Fionn's first great deeds is to slay a goblin who attacks the court of Tara with fireballs every Samhain. The goblin first lulls the warriors into inaction by playing a magic harp. Fionn, however, resists its hypnotic power by placing a magical spear against his forehead. One is reminded of Odysseus and the Sirens. This immunity to a group affliction is also seen in Cu Chulainn, who is the only Ulsterman unaffected by the debilitating curse of Macha.

The hero is also capable of forbearance and respect. We see both these qualities in Cu Chulainn when he is taunted and scorned by the braggard Etarcomol. Cu Chulainn is loth to kill the man, because he is under the protection of Cu Chulainn's foster father Fergus mac Roth. Instead he neatly slices Etarcomol's clothes from his body and then shaves his head with a single stroke of his sword. Only when Etarcomol persists does Cu Chulainn cleave his skull in two. He then begs Fergus for forgiveness, prostrating himself and allowing Fergus to drive his chariot over him three times, until Fergus accepts that Etarcomol had been insufferable. Elsewhere we learn how Cu Chulainn spares the charioteer of his enemy Orlamh, assuring the man: 'I never kill charioteers.'

Honour is another prerequisite of the Celtic hero. A true hero keeps his promises – at least most of the time. We see this in a story featuring three rivals: Cu Chulainn, Connal Cernach and Laoghaire. The mischief-maker Bricriu 'the Poison-Tongued' arranges a feast and encourages each of the three to claim the right to carve the hero's portion from the roast meat. Queen Medb awards it to Cu Chulainn, but modesty is not one of the heroic virtues, and the three men continue to argue. The King of Munster fails to pacify them. Then a giant enters and challenges each man to behead him, with the proviso that he may return and behead the man himself the next evening. Connal Cernach and Laoghaire break the agreement when the giant comes back to life. Cu Chulainn alone keeps his promise and presents himself to be beheaded – only to find that the giant was in reality the King of Munster. The King announces that Cu Chulainn's honourable behaviour proves that he is indeed the greatest hero.

On another occasion, however, Cu Chulainn accepts the same king's help in a raid, the condition being a share in the spoils. When these turn out to be better than expected – three magic cows, a magic cauldron and a beautiful fairy woman – Cu Chulainn breaks his promise and is captured and humiliated by the angry king.

Geasa

One strange phenomenon in Irish legend is the *geis*, a magical prohibition or obligation placed on a great man. Failure to observe it will inevitably cause his downfall. The word *geis* is sometimes translated as 'taboo' but, unlike a taboo, a geis is personal, not tribal. Some stories tell of a hero being placed under a geis, as is the reluctant lover Diarmid by the beautiful and insistent Grainne. Although betrothed to Fionn mac Cumhail, Diarmid's now ageing captain, Grainne's heart is set on the younger man, and she places him under geis to carry her off.

He protests feebly that he cannot follow her suggested escape route because he is under geis never to leave a royal residence through a wicket gate. 'Then use your spear to vault over the wall,' she replies.

A long pursuit ensues, during which Fionn employs his powers of clairvoyance and the young lovers repeatedly outwit him. Eventually there is a partial reconciliation, but in the end Fionn's resentment gets the better of him and he tricks Diarmid into joining a boar-hunt, and thus into breaking another geis. Diarmid is gored to death by the Boar of Ben Bulben. Fionn later meets his own end after breaking a geis, that of drinking from a horn.

Occasionally a geis takes the form of a challenge, as when Cu Chulainn twists a sapling into a hoop using only one hand, and carves on it a message in Ogham for the forces of Medb and Ailill to read: 'Do not pass beyond this point, unless there is one among you able to make a hoop like this one-handed – excepting my friend Fergus.' Medb and Ailill opt to cut another path through the forest. More often the origins of the geis are obscure, although they may have been imposed, or identified, at birth by Druids. However, there does seem to be an element of totemism, in that many geasa involve animals somehow significant in the hero's life. Diarmid's geis not to hunt the boar is linked to his father's killing of a steward's son, whose corpse is enchanted into the form of the Boar of Ben Bulben. Cu Chulainn's geis not to eat dog is linked to the episode in which he earns his name by killing a guard dog and taking its place.

Curses

Closely related to geasa are curses. The *Mabinogion* includes curses, but no geasa, although this may be partly because it was put into written form at a later and more Christianized time than the texts from which most of the Irish legends come.

One of the most powerful curses in the *Mabinogion* is the triple curse which the goddess Arianrhod angrily inflicts on her son Lleu Llaw Gyffes: he will never have a name, bear arms, or take a human wife. His father Gwydion tricks Arianrhod into naming and arming Lleu, and then, with Math Mathonwy, conjures up a wife out of flowers, Blodeuwedd. Another example is found in the story of Culhwch and Olwen. Culhwch offends his stepmother by saying that he is not old enough to marry her daughter and she swears that, therefore, the only woman he can marry is Olwen, daughter of the giant Ysbaddaden. The giant sets Culhwch a catalogue of feats to perform in order to win Olwen's hand, the most challenging being to retrieve a comb from between the ears of a particularly fearsome boar.

In psychological terms, the message of this story seems to be that only when the hero has been rejected by the mother, has separated from her and gone out into the world and proved himself, can he achieve a new union with the female principle.

Cu Chulainn – a model hero

The birth of Cu Chulainn, like that of many heroes, including Christ, is mysterious. The story goes that his mother Dechtire, sister of King Conchobar of Ulster, is betrothed to a prince, Sualtam, brother of Fergus mac Roth. At the wedding feast she swallows a mayfly which lands in her wine cup. She and her fifty maidens then fall asleep and she dreams that the god Lugh tells her, 'I was that mayfly'. He changes them into a flock of birds and orders them to follow him to Brugh na Boinne. A year later Conchobar and Fergus mac Roth are led by another flock of birds to Brugh na Boinne, where they find Dechtire giving birth. With the kind of magic that normally attends a hero's birth, at the precise moment when she is delivered of a son, a mare outside gives birth to twin foals. These eventually become the chariot horses of the boy – now named Setanta, but later to become Cu Chulainn.

Cu Chulainn exhibits a number of outward signs of supernatural power, including triple-coloured hair, seven pupils in each eye and seven digits on each hand and foot. In his battle rage one eye sinks into his head so that not even a crane could reach it, while the other bulges to the size of a cauldron big enough to boil a calf. His body spins within his skin, his hair stands on end, his muscles bulge and his howl sets the local spirits howling in sympathy. Like many heroes he has a 'sidekick', a sort of alter ego or guardian spirit and messenger, Loeg, his charioteer – reminiscent of Krishna's charioteer Arjuna in the *Mahabharata*. Loeg can make Cu Chulainn's chariot invisible.

Cu Chulainn's special enemy is the Morrigan, a goddess whom he alientates when he rejects her sexual advances. On one occasion he mortally wounds her, but is tricked into healing her by his blessings when she assumes the form of a hag with a cow and allows him to drink from its udders. Although he declines the offer of sex with the Morrigan, it is not out of constancy to his wife Emer: he has several extra-marital lovers during his short life, including the fairy woman Fann and the mortal Niamh.

The downfall of Cu Chulainn

Niamh is involved in the death of Cu Chulainn, though she tries to prevent it. It occurs some years after the Cattle Raid of Cooley. Queen Medb of Connacht has never forgiven Cu Chulainn for his massive slaughter of her forces, so she seeks out the three one-eyed daughters of Calatin, who bear a special grudge against him for killing their father and their twenty-seven brothers in the space of a single afternoon. Medb encourages them to travel far and wide learning magical arts with which to entrap Cu Chulainn. They return having learnt how to create visions of battle. Medb also enlists the support of two other enemies of Cu Chulainn – Lugaid and Erc, and tells them to gather their armies.

Conchobar learns of Medb's plan, but the men of Ulster are suffering from the curse of Macha at the time (see page 23), and are unable to help. When Conchobar's messenger arrives, Cu Chulainn is firing slingshots at birds, and missing – the first of many bad omens that Cu Chulainn's *hubris* makes him ignore. Conchobar gets Niamh to hide Cu Chulainn. However, the daughters of Calatin transform themselves into a roving wind and track him down, and proceed to weave spells to persuade him that battle is raging all around and that Ulster is in danger. At first, Niamh and her maidens are able to restrain him, soothing him with harp music, but then one of the daughters takes on Niamh's shape and lures him out, telling him that his family is under threat.

On the way home, more bad omens beset Cu Chulainn. His brooch falls and stabs him in the foot, he is offered wine that turns to blood and his horse weeps tears of blood. He then passes the three daughters, disguised as hags roasting a dog over a fire. They offer him meat and, at first, he refuses, but is caught between two geasa: he must not eat dog, but nor must he pass a hearth without tasting the meat that is roasting there. He eats and, immediately, loses half his strength. Nevertheless, when he is ambushed by Lugaid and Erc he puts up a good fight, but eventually receives a mortal wound from the spear of Lugaid.

Determined to the last, Cu Chulainn straps himself to a pillar stone so that he can remain upright – a pose whose powerful symbolism to Irish Republicanism is embodied in a bronze statue in Dublin's General Post Office. Only when the Morrigan (or her sister) perches on his shoulder to show that he is dead does Lugaid dare to approach. When he does, Cu Chulainn's sword falls and severs Lugaid's left hand.

The inevitability of this death is characteristic of the deaths of heroes. Cu Chulainn ignores the omens, but as a hero whose strongest urge is to defend his tribe he cannot ignore its peril, or that of his family. He tries to observe his geasa but is trapped, and then tricked by those who could not meet him on equal terms. He dies, but he dies fighting.

Application

The hero within

Celtic heroism can be applied to modern life, but it needs to be placed in a new context. As stated above, it is more helpful now to think of heroism as a willingness to confront our fears than as an absence of fear. Our fears, in fact, are the monsters and demons externalized in Celtic legend.

While we cannot all be doers of glorious deeds, we can be heroes in less ostentatious ways. Finding our 'hero within' involves a willingness to take necessary chances and be prepared to face the consequences. It also means acting as an individual – not following the herd, even when that seems the easy option. If we take the heroic path, we may find that we are given assistance.

Clearly we can learn from the Celtic hero's sense of honour and integrity, even if that nowadays means having the heroic presence of mind *not* to accept every challenge thrown at us. Some other Celtic hero-attributes are more difficult to translate into modern terms. However, with a little imagination we can transform the Celtic hero's magical weapons into our special strengths and the hero's geasa into the personal code by which we live our lives. Moreover, while we may not believe literally in omens, we can take a step back from our lives to observe the direction in which they are heading. We can choose to seize opportunities, yet not to tempt fate.

Chapter 5

Appearance and reality

For the Celts there was no divorce between the material and the spiritual. Their wisdom lay in perceiving the spiritual force imbuing the natural world. The physical world was in a sense insubstantial, and subject to change – a view which echoes that of Buddhism and which is borne out by science's discovery that material form is really an unceasing dance of subatomic particles. Moreover, for the Celts there were gateways leading from the material into the spiritual world. These were meeting points of appearance and reality and the key to understanding them lies in the power of symbol.

We tend to think of symbolism as an intellectual code, with only a theoretical connection between the symbol and its meaning, but it is probable that to the Celtic imagination, symbol and meaning were much closer. We see this in Celtic divination, the basis of which is twofold. First, all things are interconnected; second, nothing is merely what it seems – the physical is simply the most concrete form of the spirit. Hence a gifted Druid was able to read information about one part of the world in another part of that world: a raven flying overhead might shed light on the likely outcome of a battle. Further, a raven, while on one level being just a raven, on another might be the Morrigan.

Shield boss found in Thames, with bird heads

We see these same levels of appearance and reality in the imagery of Celtic poetry (see page 71), and perhaps even more clearly in visual art. The Celtic designs of interlaced knotwork, spirals and other motifs are formed of unbroken lines symbolizing the spiritual path of man. The spiral, in particular, was a symbol of eternal life. Celtic art was deliberately conceived in abstract form to mirror the fluidity of all life forms. Where animals, birds or humans appear they are subsumed into the pattern and illustrate the interconnectedness of all life forms. Just as the early Celts never fixed the attributes of their gods because they were often interchangeable, so their art reflects their belief in the ability of humans to partake of the wisdom and characteristics of animals and birds. It also supports their belief in shape-shifting or form-changing which was practised by the gods in the myths and also by the Druids.

Shape-shifting

The Druids not only had the ability to move between the worlds but also to shape-shift, usually into animal form – or at least to persuade themselves and others that they had done so. The filid wore cloaks made of bird feathers or of grey or white bull-hide to signal their affinity with the powers of the animal kingdom. In the myths gods would usually shape-shift into their totem animal, which is why the Morrigan often appeared as a raven. Elsewhere in the myths shape-shifting is part of a rite of passage leading to greater spiritual understanding.

One typical shape-shifting tale is that of Tuan mac Caraill – who is supposed to have lived through the successive invasions of Ireland. As an old man he went to sleep and awoke as a stag. He then lived out a life as a stag, then as a boar, a hawk and a salmon – in which form he was caught and eaten by Cairell's wife. There are also stories in which a deity is reborn from a mortal woman after she has drunk enchanted well-water or swallowed a worm. Similarly, there is the tale of Friuch and Rucht, who fight in a succession of animal forms, eventually becoming worms which are swallowed by two cows, who then give birth to the Whitehorn and the Brown Bull of Cualinge.

The tale of Blodeuwedd, the flower bride

The story of Blodeuwedd from the Welsh *Mabinogion* illustrates the use of shape-shifting and the magical powers of illusion practised by the magician Gwydion. This tale forms the fourth branch of the *Mabinogion*. In it the great king Math is magically constrained so that, except in times of war, he must rest his feet in the lap of a virgin. Math's nephew Gilvaethwy lusts after Math's virgin foot-holder and enlists the help of his magician brother Gwydion to help him ravish her. So Gwydion gets Math out of the way by provoking a war with Prideri, a neighbouring king. When Math realizes he has been tricked he punishes his two nephews by changing them into a deer and a stag and forcing them to stay in this shape for a year during which time they produce a fawn. At the end of the year he changes them into a boar and a sow who then return at the end of the year with a piglet. The third year he turns them into wolves and they return with a wolf-cub. After this he considers their punishment completed and changes them and their three offspring back into human form. Their punishment has therefore involved not only being changed into animals but also alternately into male and female. It is clear that Math regards this experience as more than a punishment, but a way of their receiving enlightenment, for he restores them absolutely after this and even asks Gwydion's advice about who to take as a replacement virgin. Gwydion suggests his sister Arianrhod.

Arianrhod fails the virginity test, which involves stepping over Math's wand and gives birth immediately to two babies. The first swims away in the sea but the second is fostered by Gwydion and is probably his own child. Although this would suggest incest we are dealing here with humanized (euhemerized) gods which puts them in the sphere of symbol. The fact that Arianrhod is associated with the moon and stars and Gwydion with the sun suggests a powerful conjunction of forces which issue in the hero child. In her anger at being cheated and humiliated Arianrhod denies her son the three initiations that should come from the mother to send him into manhood. First she refuses to name him, then she refuses to arm him, and lastly she denies his right to a human bride. The story proceeds with a battle of powers between Gwydion and Arianrhod which could be seen as the battle between the old order dominated by female powers and the new patriarchal order. Gwydion uses his powers of shape-shifting and illusion to secure these rights for his son. He changes himself and the boy into an old shoe-maker and his apprentice and when Arianrhod congratulates the boy on his skill with a catapult she finds she has inadvertently named him 'Lleu of the skilful hand'. She is similarly tricked by Gwydion when he and Lleu arrive at her castle disguised as bards. Gwydion then raises an illusory fleet of ships against her and she is tricked into arming her disguised son.

Dealing with the third curse is, however, more difficult and Gwydion is obliged to enlist the services of his magician uncle. Together they create a wife out of flowers for him, using meadowsweet, oak and broom. Blodeuwedd is no illusion; she has truly been transformed from the plant kingdom into a mortal being. She must surely be linked with the earth goddess who is allied to the land. The story continues with her betrayal of Lleu by taking another lover with whom she plots Lleu's death. Gwydion has placed a complicated protective spell on Lleu to safeguard his life, but Blodeuwedd, with the help of her lover, outwits Gwydion and kills Lleu. But at the point of death Lleu is transformed into an eagle. After much suffering he is found by Gwydion, who changes him back into human form and brings about his healing.

Blodeuwedd is not simply the hard-hearted wife; she is part of the ancient ritual involving the sacrificial death and regeneration of the king. Lleu's death is therefore part of a seasonal cycle and all the machinations of the characters in the story are an attempt at humanizing this process. In the story the powers of magical transformation are shown at different levels. Gwydion is adept at creating transitory illusions for his own purposes but when he needs to create something more lasting he has to call upon the more ancient powers symbolized by Math.

By the end of the story, Gwydion's facility for shallow trickery has evolved into real bardic power. In order to reclaim the soul of Lleu from the wounded eagle he has to call on all the power of Druidic art. He uses music and poetry in a strong combination by singing three englyns – magical verses – in order to reclaim his son. The story ends with recrimination and punishment. Blodeuwedd's lover is killed by Lleu, the returning king, and Blodeuwedd is turned into an owl. This transformation into the wise bird of the night is suggestive of the 'Mother, Maiden, Crone' motif associated with the goddess – the crone representing the wisdom of old age. Blodeuwedd is, therefore, the impersonal face of nature.

Taliesin

Another Welsh story which is rich in shape-shifting and transformation is that of Taliesin. It begins with the symbol of a cauldron of inspiration. Ceridwen desires to give her ugly son Afagddu (pronounced 'Avagthee') the gifts of wisdom and knowledge. She brews a magical potion in her cauldron and sets her steward Gwion Bach to stir it for a year and a day. Towards the end of this time, three drops spring out on to his thumb and, without thinking, he puts his thumb in his mouth. These three drops turn out to be those of knowledge, divine wisdom and inspiration, and possession of these automatically transforms him into a poet with the attendant power of shape-changing. He flees to escape the wrath of Ceridwen and goes through a series of shape-changes (see page 12). These take him symbolically through the realms of earth, water, air and fire. Becoming a grain of corn he is gobbled up by Ceridwen who has turned herself into a hen. She later gives birth to him and because of his beauty refrains from killing him, instead casting him into the sea in a leather bag. He is fished out by Elphin, son of a neighbouring king, who names him Taliesin because of his 'radiant brow'. Taliesin becomes a distinguished bard and is responsible for the great poem of being and becoming all things, the Welsh equivalent of the Irish Song of Amergin (see page 72):

> *Primary chief bard am I to Elphin,*
> *And my original country is the region of the summer stars;*
> *Idno and Heinin called me Merddin,*
> *At length every being will call me Taliesin.*
>
> *I was with my Lord in the highest sphere,*
> *On the fall of Lucifer into the depth of hell;*
> *I have borne a banner before Alexander;*
> *I know the names of the stars from north to south ...*

Rolleston

And, from the *Cad Goddau*:

> *I have been in many shapes*
> *Before I assumed a constant form:*
> *I have been a narrow sword,*
> *A drop in the air,*
> *A shining bright star,*
> *A letter among words*
> *In the book of origins ...*

Matthews, *Taliesin*

He shows his mystical identification with all ages, all realms, human, animal, physical. His bardic power is ageless – he is a type of Merlin. He moves from the bardic into the Christian age. The astonishing span of imaginative reflection contained in such poems demonstrates the scope of Celtic understanding of the interconnectedness of all things seen and unseen.

Application

Discovering symbols

An appreciation of symbology leads to higher levels of understanding on an intuitive level. The world around us is charged with meaning in symbolic form. Some central symbols have been transmuted into legends. Thus the cauldron has become the grail of Arthurian legend, symbolizing the quest for spiritual fulfilment.

To begin to rediscover the powers of shape-shifting and symbols, practise seeing shapes in abstract or natural forms. Clouds, tree roots, vegetables, markings in stones, on tree bark, or in swirling water, accidental ink blots, or anything scattered randomly by hand – are all capable of taking on symbolic form. Then consider what the symbols you see mean for you personally.

Chapter 6

The wheel of the year

To the Celts, time was circular rather than linear. This is reflected in their commencing each day, and therefore each festival, at dusk rather than dawn, a custom comparable with that of the Jewish Sabbath. It is also reflected in their year beginning with the festival of Samhain on 31 October, the time when nature appears to be dying down. Tellingly, the first month of the Celtic year is Samonios, which means 'seed fall': in other words, from death and darkness spring life and light.

Ninth-century Irish meditative figure on a bucket handle. The geometrical motifs may denote the cross of the elements, and in each corner the four elements interlocking around a swastika-like solar wheel.

Caesar confirms this and offers an explanation (*Conquest of Gaul*, VI.18):

> *The Gauls claim all to be descended from Father Dis [a god of death, darkness and the underworld], declaring that this is the tradition preserved by the Druids. For this reason they measure periods of time not by days but by nights; and in celebrating birthdays, the first of the month, and new year's day, they go on the principle that the day begins at night.*

A lunar calendar

Another reason for the importance of night in the Celts' reckoning of time lies in their regard for the moon and the feminine principle which it represents. Certainly there is some evidence that they observed the solar festivals of solstices and equinoxes, and especially the summer solstice. It is also true that the Druids' most sacred plant, mistletoe, was associated with the sun. However, the waxing and waning of the moon were of far greater importance.

The Celts showed their respect for the moon by using euphemisms such as *gealach* – meaning 'brightness' and never referring directly to 'the moon'. Manx fishermen followed this custom up until the nineteenth century, referring to the moon as *ben-reine ny hoie* – 'queen of the night'. More persuasive, however, is the evidence to be found in the Celtic calendar.

The earliest-known Celtic calendar is the Coligny calendar, now in the Palais des Arts, Lyon. It dates probably from the first century BCE, and is made up of bronze fragments, once a single huge plate. It is inscribed with Latin characters but written in Gaulish. The calendar begins each month with the full moon and covers a 30-year cycle comprising five cycles of 62 lunar months and one of 61. It divides each month into fortnights rather than weeks, with days designated – from observation – as MAT (good) or ANM (not good). Each year is divided into thirteen months.

The Coligny calendar achieves a complex synchronization of the solar and lunar months. Whether it does this for philosophical or practical reasons, it points to considerable sophistication.

The lunar months given on the Coligny calendar are as follows. The translations are based on those of Caitlin Matthews:

Samonios	October/November	Seed-fall
Dumannios	November/December	Darkest depths
Riuros	December/January	Cold-time
Anagantios	January/February	Stay-home time
Ogronios	February/March	Ice time
Cutios	March/April	Windy time
Giamonios	April/May	Shoots-show
Simivisonios	May/June	Bright time
Equos	June/July	Horse-time
Elembiuos	July/August	Claim-time
Edrinios	August/September	Arbitration-time
Cantlos	September/October	Song-time

The thirteenth lunar month, Mid Samonios, was duplicated. Since the months began with the full moon, no consistent dates can be given for them.

The Celtic festivals

We saw in Chapter 2 how when the legendary Irish hero Cu Chulainn woos Emer, he eyes her bosom and wishes aloud that he 'might wander there'. Her reply suggests the magical importance of the round of the Celtic festivals:

> No man may travel there who has not gone without sleep from Samhain to the lambing time at Imbolc, from Imbolc to the fires of Beltain, and from Beltain to the harvest time of Lughnasadh, and from then to Samhain.

This cycle is perhaps the most exciting aspect of the Celtic approach to time and, certainly, the one that we can most easily follow today. In our time, most of us are out of touch with the seasons and the one big Western festival has become more of a time for ringing tills than ringing the changes. We can bring a greater sense of rhythm and continuity into our lives by observing the Celtic festivals.

Samhain

The Celtic year began with Samhain (pronounced 'Saween'). Celebrated around 31 October, it was a time of deliberate misrule and contrariness, rather like the Roman Saturnalia. It was also a time when the veil between this world and the Otherworld was thought to be so thin that the dead could return to warm themselves at the hearths of the living, and some of the living – especially poets – were able to enter the Otherworld through the doorways of the *sidhe*, such as that at the Hill of Tara in Ireland.

At Samhain, cattle were brought in for the winter and in Ireland the warrior élite, the Fianna, gave up war until Beltain. It was a sacred time, whose peace was normally broken only by the ritualized battle of board games such as *fidchell*.

Our modern Hallowe'en stems from Samhain, and one explanation of the traditional pumpkin lanterns is that the Celts once placed the skulls of ancestors outside their doors at this time. The Christians took over the Celtic festival and turned it into All Saints Day. Even the modern English celebration of Guy Fawkes Day (Bonfire Night) on 5 November has echoes of the ancient fire festival.

Imbolc

Coming at lambing time, around 31 January, Imbolc (or Oimelc) celebrated the beginning of the end of winter. New lambs were born and a dish made from their docked tails was eaten. Women met to celebrate the return of the maiden aspect of the Goddess. This survived into Christian times as the Feast of Brigid: the saint was a Christianized version of the pagan goddess who was the daughter of the Dagda (see page 24). In the Outer Hebrides, Celtic Christian celebrations of this festival lasted into the twentieth century, with women dressing a sheaf of oats in female clothes and setting it with a club in a basket called 'Brid's Bed'.

Beltain

Beltain, celebrated around 1 May, was another fire festival; but whereas Samhain was associated with going to ground and withdrawing, Beltain burst forth with an abundant fertility. Cattle were let out of winter quarters and driven between two fires in a ritual cleansing ceremony that may have had practical purposes too. It was a time for feasts and fairs, for the mating of animals, and for divorces – possibly arising from trial marriages entered into at Lughnasadh. Like Samhain, it was a time for boardgames – as well as for travel between the worlds: the legendary poet Taliesin is said to manifest at Beltain.

Beltain was sacred to the god Belenos, the Shining One, whose name survives in place names such as Billingsgate and in Shakespeare's Cymbeline – Hound of Belenus. In fact, the word 'Beltain' derives from *Bel-tinne* – fires of Bel. As noted above, for the Fianna, Beltain heralded the start of the 'fighting season' and light is shed on this by De Jubainville, in his *Irish Mythological Cycle*:

> It was on a Thursday, the first of May, and the seventeenth day of the moon, that the [invading] sons of Miled arrived in Ireland. Partholan [chief of the next race of invaders] also landed in Ireland on the first of May … and it was on the first day of May, too, that the pestilence came which in the space of one week destroyed utterly his race. The first of May was sacred to Beltene, one of the names of the god of Death, the god who gives life to men and takes it away from them again. Thus it was on the feast day of this god that the sons of Miled began their conquest of Ireland.

Beltain is the origin of pagan May Day festivities such as those of the Padstow Hobby Horse, maypole dancing, the 'Queen of the May' and 'well dressing' – decking holy wells with flowers, as still practised in some rural communities.

Lughnasadh

Lughnasadh was a summer festival lasting for as long as two weeks either side of the day itself, which fell around 31 July. It was said to have been introduced to Ireland by the god Lugh and so was sacred to this god. The Romans identified Lugh with Mercury. At any rate, both are gods associated with skills and this festival was celebrated with competitions of skill, including horse-racing. There was horse-trading, too; perhaps this is why the festival was also linked to the fertility goddess Macha, who dies in childbirth after being forced to race against the King's horses. In Ireland the festival was associated with Emain Macha, in Ulster, but was held in various locations, including the royal fort of Tara.

Solar festivals

We know less about Celtic celebrations of solar festivals. However, the solstices were probably celebrated. Miranda Green (see Bibliography) suggests that the fires of Beltain were 'sympathetic magic to encourage the Sun's warmth on earth'. She adds that Beltain, Lughnasadh and Samhain 'celebrated critical times in the annual solar cycle', and that pagan and Christian Celtic midsummer festivals involved rolling a flaming wooden 'solar' wheel down a hill and into a river. It is also significant that sun disks, solar chariot wheels and swastikas (whose arms are intended to portray a blazing, spinning sun) are important motifs in Celtic art.

Celtic astrology and tree calendars

Astrology is an art, or science, that focuses on the passage of time and which emphasizes the unique nature of a moment in time. Much has been written about 'Celtic astrology'. Classical writers – including Strabo, Caesar, Diodorus Siculus, Cicero and Pliny – comment on Druidic knowledge of astronomy and astrology. There is also evidence that the Druids understood the tides and that they cut mistletoe and other plants at particular phases of the moon. Peter Berresford Ellis (see Bibliography) puts forward a tentative case for a Celtic astrology mentioning, among other things, the survival of astronomical terms such as *dubaraith*, meaning eclipse, into modern Irish. He suggests that if the Druids did use astrology in addition to various forms of divination, their astrology would have been lunar-based, as is Hindu astrology, which uses a system of 27 or 28 lunar 'mansions'. Another tantalizing point is the Coligny calendar's designation of days as 'good' or 'not good'. However, in the end there is no absolute proof, probably because of the Druidic aversion to keeping written records.

Similarly, there is no proof that the Ogham-based Celtic tree calendar popularized by Robert Graves actually existed, whatever poetic truth it contains.

Application

Attuning to time cycles

There are several ways to apply the Celtic sense of time. First, we can attempt to become more aware of the truth of constant change. Nothing stays the same; 'what goes around comes around'. There are 'good' days and 'not good' days. We should not cling to good times, or despair during bad times. One way to develop an awareness of this is to keep a diary of our moods and experiences. Reading it back later will develop a sense of perspective.

Keeping a diary can usefully be tied in with observing the phases of the moon – preferably in the night sky. Many people who keep a 'moon diary' find a pattern in their lives, and in their moods, corresponding to the lunar phases. This can enable you to plan accordingly, as well as developing your sense of natural rhythm.

On the larger scale, we can observe the festivals and attune our lives to seasonal changes. We may find that Samhain is a good time to become more introspective and plant the seeds of new projects, allowing them to germinate over the winter months. On a more sombre note, this is a good time to remember the dead. Beltain, on the other hand, is a time to embark on projects requiring courage and energy.

Chapter 7

The Otherworld

Mythology reveals a universal longing for a lost paradise in a time without death or suffering, when the world was more beautiful, and when humanity was closer to the gods – a time before the Fall. Plato described this longing as 'divine homesickness'. We can interpret this paradise historically; we can see it psychologically, in terms of blissful infantile oneness with the mother and with our experience; or we can see it as a spiritual longing for something ever-present but out of reach. The Celts have always had this longing in abundance and we see it in their stories of the Otherworld.

In British and Irish Celtic tales, the Otherworld is a beautiful and happy land of feasting, hunting and love-making, like this world but in a perfected form. In this it resembles the Muslim Paradise more than the Christian heaven. As one of the fairy women enticingly promises the hero Bran, it is:

> *A beauty of a wondrous land, whose aspects are lovely,*
> *Whose view is a fair country, incomparable in its haze.*

Although the Otherworld is always deathless, there can be 'trouble in paradise'. Factions form, battles are fought, and human help is enlisted. We see this when the Welsh king Pwll offends Arawn, the King of the Welsh Otherworld, by setting his dogs on a stag hunted by the Otherworldly king. Pwll has to make amends by trading places for a year and defeating Arawn's enemy Hafgan in single combat. Despite their magical powers the Otherworld beings still need human assistance.

Under earth, over sea

The Otherworld's location is mysterious. Some tales place it underground, which probably stems from an ancient respect for chthonic gods. In the Irish stories there is also a link to the past and to the ancestors. The Otherworld is populated by the Tuatha de Danann, the divine race who ruled Ireland before being driven underground into the *sidhe*.

The *sidhe*, or burial mounds, were gateways to the Otherworld. It is when Pwll sits on the mound of Gorsedd Arberth, hoping 'to see a wonder', that he first sees the Otherworldly woman Rhiannon, who is impossible to catch despite the slow pace of her horse. When Etain is discovered by her former divine husband, Midhir, he spirits her away to his *sidhe*, wherein is a land of eternal youth and feasting.

In some tales the Otherworld co-exists with this one. In the terms of modern physics it is a 'parallel universe'. Sometimes a mortal arrives there by forgetting himself in pursuit of a magical beast, as in the story of Pwll and Arawn. Cormac goes in search of his family, after exchanging them for a branch of golden apples, and enters the Otherworld through a mist – often associated with crossing over. When Oisin rides away with Niamh of the Golden Hair, they pass 'into a golden haze in which Oisin lost all knowledge of where he was, or if sea or dry land lay beneath his horse's hooves'.

Water is a symbol for the unconscious, and for the spirit, so it is not surprising to find the Otherworld often located beneath or beyond a lake. When the fairy man Fiachna appeals to Loegaire and his men to help him retrieve his abducted wife, they all dive into Loch Naneane, where the men find wonders – as well as fairy wives. Frequently the Otherworld is across the sea, and a whole class of Irish stories, the *immrama*, deal with voyages there. The journey is always westwards, to where the sun sets – the sun symbolizing the conscious self, and is usually to an Island of the Blessed. Sometimes a complicated route is followed from one island to another. Caitlin Matthews (see Bibliography) believes that these stories were intended to help the soul find its way in the afterlife and that the story of 'The Voyage of Maelduin' provides a map of the Otherworld. This theory suggests a similarity between the *immrama* and the *Tibetan Book of the Dead*, at least in purpose.

Of equal interest is the story of Bran. While crossing the sea he encounters the god Manannan mac Lir who tells him that 'Mag Mell', the Otherworld, is all around. The sea is a flowery meadow but, as yet, Bran is unable to see it. This points to two things: first, that the Otherworld is ever-present but can only be seen when we have opened 'the doors of perception'; second, that a spiritual journey contains its own destination. In a sense, we have already arrived.

Love between the worlds

Although Otherworld tales occasionally feature fairy men asking for martial assistance from mortal warriors, it is more often fairy women who tempt human heroes across the threshold. Known as *bean-sidhe* (women of the *sidhe*), or banshees, these women are incomparably beautiful. They offer love and eternal youth in a land without sorrow.

Some men, like Conle the Redhaired, struggle to resist. In Conle's case a Druid's spell at first counters the woman's, but she throws him an apple as she leaves. He touches no food but this apple for a month. He yearns for the woman and, when she returns, he tells his father: 'It is not easy for me, for I love my people; yet longing for the woman has seized me.' He sails away with her in a glass boat and is never seen again.

Once a man has tasted the delights of the Otherworld – whether its food or its women, he returns to this world at his peril. Oisin, son of Fionn, discovers this. After three weeks he starts to miss Ireland and his comrades. His lover warns him that if he sets foot on earthly soil, he will never return to the Land of Youth. He rides home and is amazed at the stunted nature of the men he sees. As he leans from his horse to move a rock for them, his saddle girth breaks, and he falls to the ground. At once he ages 300 years – the length of earth-time that has passed since his departure to the Otherworld. Others who return from the Otherworld become ashes at the moment they alight, although this probably only signifies the death that would have occurred naturally when more time had passed.

This slowness of time in the Otherworld has parallels in modern physics. Time is slowed down by gravity. Gravity increases as one approaches the core of a mass, so time runs more slowly towards the earth's centre. Some physicists, including Stephen Hawking, believe that time travel could be possible in black holes, where gravity warps time and space. Moreover, time slows down as one nears the speed of light. Owing to this, astronauts who have been to the moon have, as a result, aged slightly less than they would have done on earth. It is just possible that these Otherworld journeys show an intuitive knowledge, if not a memory, of such undulations in the fabric of time.

Another way to interpret the Otherworldly time warp is in terms of consciousness. The Otherworld could signify a return to childhood consciousness, with all its magical intensity. When one is focused on the moment, time can almost stand still. One way to achieve this focus and apparent suspension of time, is through music, which features strongly in descriptions of the Otherworld. Mortals who go there are enchanted by 'sweet music striking the ear', often in the form of song, which could be produced by women or birds. Moreover, the people of the Otherworld love music so much that they sometimes even abduct musically gifted mortals to play for them.

For the Celts, music also had magical effects in this world. There is a story of the Dagda's harp which was captured by the Fomorians at the Battle of Moytura. The Dagda went after it and found it in the hall of Bres. He called it to him and it immediately came to his hand across the hall, killing nine men on the way. He then commanded it in verse to play the three noble strains, *goltrai*, *gantrai* and *seantrai*, or the sad, happy and sleep strains. Leaving all assembled in the hall fast asleep he stole away with his harp. The properties of these different musical moods were probably bound up with the use of musical keys.

Animus, anima and soul loss

One very interesting tale of love between the worlds is that of 'The Wasting Sickness of Cu Chulainn'. One Samhain, the great protector of Ulster ignores the advice of his charioteer Loeg and casts slingshots at two birds whose origins are clearly Otherworldly: their song has lulled the other Ulstermen to sleep. Cu Chulainn angrily aims his spear, but the birds disappear into a lake.

Soon Cu Chulainn falls asleep and has a vision in which he is scourged by two laughing fairy women. He then falls into a sickness so grave that he cannot even speak for a year. A fairy man, Angus, brings the message that one of the women – the man's sister Fann – is in love with Cu Chulainn and that the hero can be healed in the Otherworld.

Returning to the place of his vision, Cu Chulainn meets another sister, Liban. She tells him that Fann's husband, the god Manannan mac Lir, has abandoned Fann and that Fann has set her heart on Cu Chulainn. Liban's husband, Labraid the Swift Sword-Wielder, offers Fann to the hero in return for a day's service in battle. With uncharacteristic caution, Cu Chulainn sends Loeg ahead to reconnoitre. Loeg reports favourably. When Liban invites Cu Chulainn to go with her, Cu Chulainn again sends his trusty charioteer in his place. Loeg here represents the protective part of the psyche that makes a detached assessment of the situation before the whole person plunges in.

Finally Cu Chulainn goes, and enjoys the favours of Fann for a month before her right to him is fiercely contested by his wife Emer, backed up by her retinue of women. Both Fann and Emer offer to give up Cu Chulainn, but he chooses Emer. Nevertheless when Fann goes back to Manannan, Cu Chulainn goes mad with longing, until given a drink of forgetfulness, which is also given to Emer, 'that she might forget her jealousy'.

Caitlin Matthews (see Bibliography) identifies this story with 'soul loss': Cu Chulainn loses his soul when scourged – an act with shamanic associations – and, again, when Fann leaves him. Another interpretation is in terms of Jung's concept of *animus* and *anima*. For a man, the anima is a potent but undeveloped inner 'female' part of his psyche that he projects onto a woman when 'falling in love'. The animus is its corresponding opposite in a woman. The *bean-sidhe* may be seen as anima figures; they are captivating, and offer a way to the Otherworld and an enrichment of the psyche, but they can also rob a man of his power to act in the material world. It is interesting that there are no Celtic tales of women entering the Otherworld.

J. A. MacCulloch (see Bibliography) offers an intriguing slant on Otherworldly love. He suggests that the mythical Islands of Women stem from a time when women performed their rites in seclusion. 'To these rites men may have been admitted by favour, but perhaps to their detriment, because of their temporary partner's extreme erotic madness.' In other words, the heroes were not so much homesick as overwhelmed!

The Celts and reincarnation

Archaeological finds testify to a strong Celtic belief in a physical afterlife. On the Continent, especially, there have been excavations of burials in which people of rank have been interred with weapons, utensils, ornaments, food and drink – for use in the next world. In the early centuries CE, cremation became popular, but grave goods were still buried with the ashes. In Britain there were relatively few burials, except in the north-east; it is likely that corpses were exposed until the soul was thought to have departed, and then the bones disposed of, rather as in Tibetan Buddhist 'sky' burials.

Classical authors comment on the Celts' belief in reincarnation, or 'transmigration' of the soul. Diodorus Siculus writes:

> *Among them the doctrine of Pythagoras prevailed that the souls of men were immortal, and after completing their term of existence they live again, the soul passing into another body. Hence at the burial of the dead some threw letters addressed to dead relatives on the funeral pyre, believing that the dead would read them in the next world. (V.28)*

The letters are suspect – the Celts were not literate. But more than this, there is little evidence for belief in reincarnation to be found in the myths. Some authors point to shape-shifting tales (see page 39) and cite the god figure on the Gundestrup cauldron who appears to be dipping a warrior in a restorative cauldron. There is even some suggestion in the myths that the seventh-century Irish king Mongan was an incarnation of the god Manannan mac Lir, previously born as Fionn mac Cumhail. However, none of this constitutes evidence for belief in reincarnation for ordinary mortals.

The myths suggest that heroes go to the Otherworld when they die, but not that they return. If the Celts believed in reincarnation, why are there no stories about children being recognized as incarnations of ancestors, or heroes from the past? There is certainly no evidence of individual Celts striving to secure a favourable reincarnation by good deeds in this life. It is possible that the Romans and Greeks interpreted Celtic belief in resurrection in the more familiar context of Pythagoras' doctrine of transmigration. Another possibility is that the Celts saw the Otherworld as a temporary resting-place for the soul before it once again took on earthly form. We can at least be certain that although the Otherworld in some ways resembles the Christian heaven, there was for the Celts no concept of hell or damnation.

Application

Love and the Otherworld

We all need ideals — for our own conduct and in our relationships; but it is possible to become lost in them. Perhaps our romantic ideal is so strong that we cannot love a real person, or we idealize a past partner, with the same result. Or else we repeatedly fall in love and project the ideal – animus or anima – on to a partner. For a while we live in an enchanted Otherworld, only to find our love turns to ashes when we return to earth. Perhaps like Cu Chulainn we need to exercise caution and retain some initial detachment. We may also need to accept that the ideal exists only in our imagination – yet be prepared to search for its potential in a real-life partner.

In a more general sense, we should explore the concept that the magic of the Otherworld is all around us if we look and listen – a source of joy and inspiration that can be contacted by patient observation and stilling of the mind.

Chapter 8

The Druids

Diodorus Siculus said of the Druids: 'They are of much sincerity and integrity, far from the craft and knavery of men among us, contented with homely fare, strangers to excess and luxury.'

The Druids were the intelligentsia of the Celtic peoples. They were also their 'holy' men or women, guardians of a high wisdom and knowledge. Their position was, therefore, similar to that of the Brahmin caste in India. The Irish word *drui* means 'oak' and the Druid was 'one who has knowledge of the oak'. The Druids were poets, teachers, philosophers, seers, mages and judges, keepers of the history of the people and of ancient magical lores.

The origins of the Druids are unknown but some scholars believe that they were an ancient people who came from the West and that it was these proto-Druids who built the ancient stone circles and later merged with the incoming Celtic peoples. Whether this is true or not, it is a fair assumption that they used some of the sacred stone circles for their rituals.

But there is a more imaginative tale concerning their origins which tells how they were once magicians dwelling on the Island of Atlantis. In time some of them began turning to the black arts as a result of which the island became supernaturally threatened by flood. The dark lords were engulfed as the island sank below the sea but the white lords, owing to their superior power and foreknowledge, managed to escape and journeyed both east and west to the lands of Britain and America. However fanciful this story, it is certainly true that Britain later became known as the seat of Druidic lore and all serious students had to journey there for instruction.

More authoritatively, we have Caesar's and other classical accounts of the Druids' role in Celtic society. From these sources we know that they held supreme power over the Celts, even over kings, and that they officiated at religious rituals. We also know that they acted as judges in both civil and religious matters, were subordinate to a head Druid and were exempt from military service and payment of taxes.

Strabo, writing in the first century BCE, divides the Druids into three main categories: '…the Bards are singers and poets; the Vates, diviners and natural philosophers; while the Druids, in addition to natural philosophy, study also moral philosophy' (4.4.4). These three qualifications required distinct periods of training.

Bards

The bards were poets who immersed themselves in the sacred power of the word. Their function was also to maintain an oral memory of tribal history. Ammianus says: 'the Bards sang to the sweet strains of the lyre the valorous deeds of famous men composed in heroic verse' (15.9.8). Such performances were a high art and the result of a rigorous training. The bards were skilled in the art of music as a setting for the sagas and also as a means of influencing the emotions of their hearers, famously with the three musical strains (see Chapter 7).

The Celts were forbidden by their religion to write down any of their teachings, probably because of the high value they placed on the Word. The Druids believed that the Truth was enshrined in the Word and that the Word was, therefore, divine and needed to be protected. Moreover, their work lay in 'searching into secret and sublime things' (Ammianus 15.9.8). Their philosophy was therefore of a high order and they wished to protect it from distortion or falling into the wrong hands. Bards underwent a twelve-year training during which they memorized numerous poems and some 350 stories as well as studying poetic form, grammar, the Law of Privileges, prophetic invocation, orations and the Ogham alphabet. At the same time a bard was also expected to be a source of inspiration.

Accommodation in bardic colleges was deliberately severe because it was believed that sensory deprivation aided poetic inspiration. In order to compose a poem, bards would lie on the floor in the dark with stones on their stomachs to prevent them becoming drowsy. The development of memory combined with the inspirational dedication to the sacred word gave rise to strong inner powers bordering on those of the ovate and Druid. This was particularly true of the Irish *filid*, the poet-seers.

The powers of the bard combined with those of the ovate in the composition of *Dindsenchas* or place-name stories. It was the function of the poet to know the history of every important place. If the history of a place was unknown the poet was required to find out about it by means of a divinatory dream.

Bronze, silver or gold branches marked different levels of achievement. When reciting poetry the bard or fili would carry a branch hung with bells which would attract attention and magically summon inspiration from the Otherworld. The branch was a symbol of the strength and energy of poetic creation and was allied to the Otherworldly tree believed to grow in the Blessed Islands of the West.

The Word was magically potent. By composing a *glam dicin*, or poetic satire, a bard could ruin a man. An example of this in *The Book of Invasions* tells how King Bres was satirized by the bard Corpry for his lack of hospitality and as a result was forced to abdicate. The power of satire could also cause physical harm such as boils on the face or barrenness in animals or the land. But bardic incantations were more regularly used to exalt the history of the tribe, praise patrons or invoke the Otherworld.

Ovates

Some bards continued their training and became ovates. Ammianus calls them 'Euhages' and says they investigated the sublime and 'attempted to explain the secret laws of nature'. They were seers and prophets whose special role lay in divination.

One of their practices, *Imbas Forosna*, required them to chew the flesh of a totem animal in order to receive its wisdom, after which they would fall asleep attended by watchers. In this way they would receive a prophetic dream concerning the whole tribe. Other types of divination included psychometry – the ability to ascertain the history of an object through touch. Most appropriately there was *Teinm Laeghda*, 'illumination through poetry' in which the truth would be revealed by the spontaneous composition of a poem. Other forms of divination included observation of natural phenomena such as shapes of clouds or flames, the flight or songs of birds and the reckoning of auspicious and inauspicious days, as evidenced in the Coligny calendar (see Chapter 6).

The ovates were also herbalists and healers, possessing a strong knowledge of animal and tree lore. They were shamanic, being able to move between the two worlds of the temporal and spiritual. Their wooden staves were often carved with Ogham inscriptions believed to be used in divination.

The Ogham alphabet

Because of their strict belief in the oral tradition, the Druids left no written text. But they did use a symbolic alphabet known as Ogham (pronounced O'um). It consisted of twenty-five strokes to either side of a central line. It was engraved on wood or stone. Each line or series of lines represented a letter of the alphabet. The Ogham letters were also linked with the names of trees, as shown opposite. Similarly there were systems using the names of birds, rivers, colours or even food. Ogham inscriptions can be found today on standing stones, chiefly in Ireland.

THE OGHAM ALPHABET

Letter	Irish name	Tree
B	beith	birch
L	luis	rowan
F	fearn	alder
S	saille	willow
N	nuinn	ash
H	huathe	hawthorn
D	duir	oak
T	tinne	holly
C	coll	hazel
Q	quert	apple
M	muinn	vine
G	gort	ivy
NG	ngetal	broom/fern (reed)
STR	straif	blackthorn
R	ruis	elder
A	ailm	fir/pine
O	onn	gorse
U	ur	heather
E	edhadh	aspen
I	ido	yew
EA	ebhadh	aspen
OI	oir	spindle
UI	uileand	honeysuckle
IO	iphin	gooseberry
AE	phagos	beech

Druids

The Druids were those who had achieved the highest grade in the caste, having trained for twenty years and become philosophers and teachers, especially of astronomy and the natural sciences. Caesar tells us they 'hold long discussions about the heavenly bodies and their movements, the size of the universe and of the earth, the physical constitution of the world, and the power and properties of the gods; and they instruct the young men in all these subjects' (VI.14).

The Druids, however, were not simply mystics. Rather, they were religious leaders with considerable secular authority who married and had children, held sovereignty over kings, performed at all religious sacrifices and acted as judges.

Brehons

Strabo said 'The Druids are considered the most just of men'. The Druid judges were known as Brehons. They compiled an ancient code of law known as the Brehon laws which were later transcribed into the *Seanchus Mor*, a system of Irish law. The Brehon laws confirm the high status accorded to Celtic women compared to their position among the Greeks and Romans. Women could be Brehons, and Brigid famously held this role. The Brehons presided over all disputes and meted out the appropriate penalties. Their most serious punishment – and the one most feared – was banning a tribe or individual from taking part in sacrifice to the gods. Anyone thus excluded would be unable to enter the Otherworld at death. Sometimes they used forms of divination such as *crannchur*, or casting wooden lots, as a means of judgment. Again, the power of truth was central to judgment.

Although exempt from military service, Druids were strongly influential in war. Often when the armies were drawn up, they would go between the lines and stop the battle by means of arbitration. At other times they would be at the battle scene using supernatural powers against the enemy, invoking curses or visiting physical afflictions on them. A typical posture adopted for cursing the enemy was standing on one leg, with one arm held out and one eye closed. This posture was adopted by the god Lugh in the Battle of Moytura. A dramatic account is given by Tacitus of the Druids' last stand on Anglesey in 64 CE in which they were seen 'raising their hands to heaven and screaming dreadful curses' while black-robed Druidesses 'like Furies', their wild hair streaming, brandished torches (*Annals*, xiv 26). The Druids could also appropriate the forces of nature and raise storms, mists and snowfalls against the enemy.

Beliefs

The central tenet of Druidic philosophy has been summarized as 'To honour the gods, to do no evil and to practise courage'. They taught that the soul and the universe were both indestructible but that 'fire and water must one day prevail'. They taught in riddles and allusion, dialogue and verse, drawing on the observation of nature to illustrate spiritual and philosophical concepts. An indication of their teaching is given in the following riddling poem:

> *What is sweeter than mead? – Intimate conversation.*
> *What is blacker than the raven? – Death.*
> *What is whiter than snow? – Truth.*
> *What is swifter than the wind? – Thought.*
> *What is sharper than the sword? – Understanding.*
> *What is lighter than a spark? – The mind of a woman*
>   *between two men.*

Berresford-Ellis, from *The Druids*

Ritual

The Celts preferred to worship in nature, rather than in man-made temples, and it was only after the coming of the Romans that they built any substantial temples. The oak was sacred to the Druids, being one of the oldest trees and therefore representing tradition, continuity and wisdom. The Druids, as holders of oak-wisdom, possessed an ancient and sacred knowledge handed down through the generations. They alone were permitted to officiate at ceremonies which were commonly held in sacred groves of oak trees.

Pliny describes a ritual in which mistletoe is ceremonially cut from a grove of oak trees by a Druid using a golden sickle. It is not allowed to touch the ground, but is caught in a white sheet, after which two white bulls are offered as sacrifice and prayers are made for prosperity. The mistletoe was considered sacred because it grew out of the oak, never having touched the ground. It therefore symbolized the divine spark of creativity, also of fertility because of the consistency of the juice of its white berries. This ritual was generally performed at the winter solstice, a time when the longest night began to yield to the return of the light, thus promising a renewal of life and fertility after the apparent death of the sun and nature. The golden sickle was also an important combined symbol of sun and moon.

Sacrifices

Sacrifice of animals was a feature of all important festivals but classical writers also give accounts of human sacrifice. Two reasons were offered for this. One concerned the offering of life for life in the case of a person who was sick, the other 'haruspicy', a method of divination deriving from an interpretation of the death-throes of the victim, who was often a convicted criminal.

The practice of human sacrifice was the main reason Romans gave for outlawing the Druids during the conquest of Britain. It was so effective as anti-Druid propaganda that it has discredited the Druids ever since. While it would be foolish to suggest that such sacrifices never occurred, it is worth noting that there is little evidence of it other than in the classical writings. There is very little mention of it in the mythical cycles or in the Lives of the Saints, where it would have served as a useful tool for the monks in their fight against paganism. Archaeological evidence is also surprisingly sparse, compared to that for Greek and Roman human sacrifice. The superbly preserved Lindow Man (see page 12) is perhaps the strongest example of human sacrifice. Others include skeletons in the foundations of important buildings on sacred sites.

Because the Druids had such authority over the Celtic peoples, they constituted a very potent political threat to Roman occupation, being able to galvanize intertribal support from the

Celts. As the intelligentsia they were powerfully subversive in their thinking, from the Roman point of view. The Druids were spiritually orientated, their beliefs being based on their mythology. Their veneration of the land prohibited land ownership and their veneration of the goddess led to their valuing women as social equals. By contrast the Romans had a materialistic and hierarchical outlook, believing in land ownership, patriarchal succession and the subjugation of women. Their outcry against Druidic human sacrifice conflicts with the fact that Rome itself was still indulging in human sacrifice on a grand scale. Their portrayal of the Druids as 'pagan' or 'heathen' was an attempt to discredit their reverence for the land and to portray them as naive. On the contrary there is every reason to suppose that the Druids were one of the most enlightened classes of people from the ancient world.

The fall of the Druids

The Romans outlawed Druidism in the first century CE and finally put it down with force as we have seen in Tacitus' description of the decisive battle of Mona (Anglesea). The Druids tried to protect their stronghold using their magic arts but the Romans pressed the attack and 'enveloped them in the flames of their own torches'. They then cut down their sacred groves. After that the Druids fled either to Ireland or north of Hadrian's Wall. Some of them took on the bardic mantle in order to avoid censure and their ritual observances and magical arts went underground.

Application

Divination

There is a fine line between using divination as a means of accessing the unconscious, allowing ideas to arise from new connections – and encouraging simple superstition. One opens up possibilities and liberates the mind; the other works through fear, and imprisons the mind with irrational worries.

The Druids used three main methods of divination. Firstly, they both summoned and interpreted dreams. By placing a notebook and pen beside your bed you can let your unconscious self know that you are ready to listen to it. Interpretation is very personal and can be achieved by attending to the symbols, puns and moods of the dream or by interrogating individual characters who appear in it.

Secondly, the Druids used their own creative skills in divination. Working directly with words or any of the creative media brings surprising results. For example, by attempting to express a problem in tight poetic metre and rhyme you will often find something extra appears in the text and suggests a solution.

Thirdly, the Druids used Ogham letters cut into strips of wood which they consulted by casting on the ground, or by drawing from a bag. All cultures have used variants on this kind of divination, of which the I Ching, the Tarot and Runes are examples. These systems attempt to make predictions from the observation of random events or patterns in nature, a technique which stems from the belief that all things are interconnected. Whether one traces pictures in the clouds or in a tea-cup, creates a sequence from Tarot cards, or throws dice or sticks, the aim is still to find meaning in the universe. Another way of looking at it is as a method of activating the right-brain when the logical left-brain has drawn a blank! Superstitious fear occurs when the right-brain is given too much power and common sense is ignored.

You could create your own Ogham alphabet on twigs or stones. Then link the letters to trees, birds, food or anything you choose. Experiment with finding your own correspondences and using your alphabet to answer questions. For example, if you choose trees, as in the table on page 63, consider what each tree means to you. Oak might suggest reliability, willow sadness, and so on. Then, ask your question and pick out three Ogham characters from a bag. Consider how they shed light on your situation.

Chapter 9

Truth, honour and justice

To the Celts, truth was not something to be altered to suit one's needs; nor was it just morally desirable: it was a sacred quality with a magical power. Moreover, truth was embodied in the word, it was the foundation of all speech. It is largely for this reason that the Druids kept no written records of their beliefs or rituals – although Caesar may be right in adding to this reason the Druids' reluctance to make their knowledge public, as well as the intellectual benefits of committing learning to memory.

The philosophical weight of Celtic belief in the power of truth is summed up in the words: 'By Truth the earth endures'. In Old Irish, the word for 'truth' shares its root with that for 'holiness'. Even in modern times Irish mourners console themselves with the idea that the deceased has gone to 'the place of Truth'.

Classical authors refer to the eloquence of the Celts and to the value which they place on words. Diodorus Siculus, on the other hand, gives us another slant on them:

> *In conversation they use few words and speak in riddles, for the most part hinting at things and leaving a great deal to be understood. They frequently exaggerate with the aim of extolling themselves and diminishing the status of others. They are boasters and threateners and given to quick bombastic self-dramatization.*

Quoted in Berresford-Ellis, *Caesar's Invasion of Britain*

Using 'few words' and 'speaking in riddles' may be the marks of a people who did not squander words and who were drawn to metaphor, or it may be that the Celts were deliberately enigmatic with the unwelcome Roman invader. However, the boastfulness referred to had a clearer purpose. When Celtic warriors met in single combat they would wage a ritualistic war of words before resorting to blows, declaring their own prowess and that of their ancestors, as well as pouring scorn on their opponent. There are even reports of contests ending at this stage. In modern times we look down on boasting, but here it serves to save lives.

The power of naming

An aspect of speech that confers special power is that of naming. To name a thing is not just to give it a label: it is to identify its true nature and to assert a relationship with it. Thus the *Dindsenchas*, the Irish place-name stories (see Chapter 2), poetically identify the Irish landscape with its gods and goddesses, with the land's memory of what has occurred in each place and they assert the relationship of the Gaels with the land. In Celtic legend the way in which a hero gets his name is similarly significant, as when the boy Setanta wins the name of Cu Chulainn, Hound of Culann, when he takes the place of Culann's guard dog, whom he has slain (see p. 33). In short, the names we give to people, or places, are always important.

The poet's power

Some of the greatest literature in English has been written by latter-day Celts. It is characterized by a sensitivity to the music of words and to the magical, shape-shifting, power of metaphor. Robert Burns, James Joyce, Dylan Thomas and R. S. Thomas follow a tradition that goes back over 2,000 years.

Poetry to the early Celts was never intended merely to entertain: it was magical and incantatory. When the Milesians came to invade Ireland and displace the Tuatha de Danann, their great poet Amergin laid claim to the land on behalf of his people by identifying himself completely with it:

I am the wind that blows over the ocean,
I am the wave of the sea,
I am the murmur of the billows.
I am the ox of the seven combats,
I am the hawk upon the crag,
I am a ray of the sun.
I am the fairest of plants,
I am a wild boar in valour,
I am a salmon in the pool,
I am a lake in the plain.
I am the craft of the artificer,
I am the word of science,
I am the spear-point that gives battle,
I am the god that creates in man the fire of thought.

Who if not I enlightens the assembly upon the mountain?
Who tells the ages of the moon?
Who shows the place where the sun goes to rest?
        adapted from De Jubainville, *Irish Mythological Cycle*

In this incantation, Amergin summons up the power of the primeval waters, of the plant and animal kingdoms, of humanity and god-inspired human intellect and of the Druids – if not the gods themselves.

There are many instances of the power of poetry in Celtic tradition. For example, in the *Mabinogion*, Gwydion literally has the power to 'charm the birds out of the trees'. Poets fulfilled an equally powerful role in orally preserving the history of the tribe's ancestors and of the land. However, if provoked they could become destructive. No great man took lightly the risk of having a satire composed against him by a disgruntled poet. Such a satire could not only ruin a man's reputation and make him a laughing-stock: it could cause him actual bodily harm (see Chapter 8), as could another form of magical incantation frequently used, the curse.

Poets could also exercise their power against each other. There are examples of poetic contests, such as that between the Irish bard Senchan Torpeist and a poetess, as he lands on the shores of the Isle of Man (given in *Cormac's Glossary*). The poetess pronounces two lines and challenges Senchan to find the next two. He is at a loss and his honour is saved only by an ugly youth who speaks the lines for him. The implication is that there are only two lines that could possibly follow; poetry is not a matter of taste, but of *le mot juste*. There is also the well-known story of the legendary Welsh bard Taliesin. As an infant he is disdained by a group of poets coming to ask their fee of the king. The young poet renders them speechless: all they can do is to make baby noises with their fingers on their open lips.

In Ireland the top poets were known as the *fili*, and their training could take twelve years. It is little wonder that they were greatly respected. One of the maxims of the Irish warrior élite, the Fianna, was: 'Show two-thirds of your gentleness to women and to those that creep on the floor [children], and to poets.' Moreover, to become one of the Fianna, a warrior had not only to pass tests of physical skill and valour, but to be expert in the Twelve Books of Poetry, and in poetic composition.

Another reason for becoming a poet was that the honour-price to be paid for slaying a poet was ruinously high. Thus when a young Fionn mac Cumhail (later captain of the Fianna) carries out a revenge killing, he is obliged to go and study poetry with the Druid Finegas in order to escape the wrath of the man's family.

Honour

A Celtic saying goes: 'A man lives after his life, but not after his honour'. The basis of this honour was truth. A man had to be true to himself, to his promises, and to his lord. Among other maxims of the Fianna are:

> *Do not speak swaggeringly, or refuse to yield what is right; it is a shameful thing to make idle threats. So long as you live, never forsake your lord, nor for gold or any other worldly reward abandon one whom you have promised to protect ... Do not carry tales or utter falsehoods.*

It seems that the shame is not so much in making a boast as in not living up to it.

Strabo speaks of the Celts' loyalty to their chieftains, but his observations show that this loyalty extends to a wider mutual support:

> *... if roused, they come together all at once for the struggle, both openly and without circumspection, so that for those who wish to defeat them by stratagem they become easy to deal with – in fact, irritate them when, where, or by what chance pretext you please, and you have them ready to risk their lives, with nothing to help them in the struggle but might and daring. ... And on account of their trait of simplicity and straightforwardness they easily come together in great numbers, because they always share in the vexation of those of their neighbours whom they think wronged. (4.4.2)*

We also see here the Celtic disdain for stratagem. What Strabo refers to as 'simplicity', the Celts themselves would see as honourable openness. Hence Keelta, a member of the Fianna, when asked by St Patrick to account for the Fianna's glory answers: 'Truth was in our hearts and strength in our arms, and what we said, that we fulfilled'. Another member of the Fianna, Conan, angers Fionn mac Cumhail by employing trickery to defeat an invader who challenges the Fianna. Conan fools the advancing invader, Liagan, with an old trick: 'Truly, you are in more peril from the man behind than from the man in front.' Liagan spins round and Conan slices off his head.

Elsewhere, particularly in the *Mabinogion*, it seems that trickery – though not outright lying – is acceptable in times of need. The magician Gwydion tricks his sister Arianrhod into giving birth as she steps over his wand to prove her virginity to the royal court. He also tricks her into naming and arming their son, Lleu Llaw Gyffes. Another hero, Pwll, is tricked into surrendering his bride Rhiannon to her former suitor, because he promises the stranger to grant whatever favour he asks. Honour forces him to keep his promise when the man asks for Rhiannon. Luckily, she tells Pwll how to get her back – by another trick. Even the great Cu Chulainn has to put the whole of Ulster at risk because he has promised to spend the night with a serving girl.

Justice

Closely related to Celtic concepts of truth and honour is that of justice. This was not something merely pragmatic. Rather, justice was divinely inspired and had a magical power. After the poet Amergin (see above) has pronounced his great invocation of the powers of Ireland, his next act is to make what is hailed as the 'first true judgment' in Ireland: namely, that the Milesians should retire and give the defending De Dananns a fair chance. A true judgment is seen as indisputable wisdom, which has mystical power, as when the young Cormac mac Art makes a true judgment in place of a king's false one, with magical consequences.

Thus in Celtic society the judges were not ordinary officials, but a branch of the Druids, the *Brehons* (see page 64). Their judgments were often inspired, either directly or through divination (see page 38), although they sometimes let the elements decide, for example by setting a suspect afloat on the sea in a boat without oar, sail or rudder. However, Celtic law became increasingly codified. In Ireland there were the Brehon Laws, in Wales the Laws of Hywel Dda and in Brittany the Breton Laws, which remained in force until 1532. In Cornwall there were the Laws of Dunwallo Molmutius (c.450 BCE), some of which probably influenced the Anglo-Saxon Laws of Alfred.

On the personal level, one recognized way of obtaining justice was to fast outside the door of the person against whom one had a grievance, to shame them into offering reparation. It is unclear how widely this was used, but it does seem to be the historical precedent for Irish Republican hunger strikes, as well as linking with Hindu practices.

If we can learn from Celtic law, it is above all from its socialist principles. Territory belonged to the tribe, with individuals having the right to work a plot of land but not to sell it. There was no absolute ownership and there were even restrictions on an individual selling cattle or other important goods. As for trespass we can take it that, at least within the tribe, the 'right to roam' existed unfettered. On the other hand, the roaming of bees was taken into account by the Irish legal code's 'Bee Judgment', whereby an owner of bees had to distribute honey to his neighbour every third year, because the pollen had been gathered from their lands. It is interesting to note that principles of common ownership survived in Scotland into the nineteenth century and as late as 1895 on the islands of Islay and St Kilda.

As to social divisions, while it cannot be said that all were equal, there was little slavery. The lowest class, that of 'non-freemen' – law-breakers, cowards, prisoners-of-war and hostages – was able to acquire land, but not vote. Above this came landless tribesmen and then the majority – land-working, tax-paying voters. Then came a civil service class responsible for public works such as organizing the local hospital and orphanage and then Druids, Bards, lawyers and doctors. This class also included chiefs – who were elected – and their immediate family.

The democratic nature of Celtic society is shown in the insistence on everyone having their say. Strabo writes:

> There is a procedure that takes place in their assemblies which is peculiar to them: if a man disturbs the speaker and heckles him, the sergeant-at-arms approaches him with drawn sword, and with a threat commands him to be silent; if he does not stop, the sergeant-at-arms does the same thing a second time, and also a third time, but at last cuts off enough of the man's 'sagus' [tunic] to make it useless for the future. (4.4.3)

The position of women

Celtic women were used to standing up for themselves. Marcellinus writes that a Celt will be more than a match for 'a whole band of foreigners ... if he call in his wife, stronger than he by far and with flashing eyes; least of all when she swells her neck and gnashes her teeth, and poising her huge white arms, proceeds to rain punches mingled with kicks, like shots discharged by the twisted cords of a catapult.' (XV, 12, 1)

Women not only went into battle, but even led armies. Boudicca, Queen of the Iceni, led a bold and initially successful revolt against Roman rule in the east of Britain (see page 30). Perhaps this helps to explain why Celtic women enjoyed a high degree of equality and independence – of which classical commentators sometimes disapproved. Both Strabo and Caesar comment on the financial independence of women. Strabo further notes that daughters could become heads of family, which he judges to be 'a sort of woman-rule ... not at all a mark of civilisation'. (3.4.18)

Application

Working with the word

The most obvious lessons that we can learn from Celtic attitudes to truth, honour and justice are moral ones. In particular, we can try to be more truthful in our lives and, especially, in those areas in which we may be inclined to regard truth as a luxury – such as business. We do not have to be brutally honest, but we can at least experiment with telling the truth in as kind and inoffensive a way as possible. The earth may not move as a result, but we may find that our personal power increases. Another lesson is that of listening to what other have to say, without butting in or pre-judging.

More mystically, we can give some time to reading and writing poetry as a way of getting in touch with the sacred use of the word. Reading poetry involves a slowing down and dwelling on the sounds of words, on their multiple levels of meaning and on their imagery, with its power to alter our perception of the world. A poetic exercise in keeping with the spirit of the Celts is to write as if you are something in nature, such as a fish, a tree, or a river. If you want to attempt the all-embracing approach of Amergin, try writing as if you are all of nature at once. Begin with what you see, hear, feel and smell in your garden, or in the countryside. Become aware of the interplay of words, and of the truth that they contain.

Chapter 10

The Celtic Church

Christianity was brought to Britain along with other religious cults by the Romans. But the most notable feature of Celtic Christianity was the monastic movement which arrived in Britain around 400 CE. According to Bede the first monastery in Britain was founded by Ninian, at Whithorn in Galloway. He was inspired by Martin of Tours who, in turn, had taken his model from the Desert Fathers and Mothers of Egypt. Martin saw monasticism as a way of evangelizing rural areas. A catechism attributed to Ninian gives his aim 'to perceive the eternal word of God reflected in every plant and insect, every bird and animal, and every man and woman'.

The monastic movement grew and flourished, particularly in the fifth and sixth centuries. In Britain it was mostly confined to the west coast, because of Saxon invasion in the east. For reasons of safety and also to foster a stricter Christian discipline, many foundations were sited on remote and inhospitable islands, such as Skellig St Michael off the west coast of Ireland. The monks lived close to nature and this was reflected in their spiritual outlook:

> *I have a hut in the wood, none knows it but my Lord; an ash tree this side, a hazel on the other, a great tree on a mound encloses it ...*

> *A clutch of eggs, honey, produce of heath-peas, God has sent it; sweet apples, red bog-berries, whortleberries ...*

Fair white birds come, cranes, seagulls, the sea sings to them,
no mournful music.

For my part I am grateful for what is given me from my dear
Christ.

Tenth-century Irish, trans. Jackson

Here is delight in the natural world and a turning of that
delight towards the Creator in exuberance and appreciation. The
mead halls are not far away, nor are the hazel-nuts of wisdom, nor
the Otherworld. The same intimacy with which the hermit
speaks of nature characterizes his relationship with Christ.

Another Irish poem says:

I should like to have a great ale-feast for the King of Kings; I
should like the Heavenly Host to be drinking it for
all eternity.

I should like to have the Three Marys of glorious renown
I should like to have the Heavenly Host from every side.

Jackson

Here the triple-aspected Celtic goddess has become Mary, the
great mother. Mary received great respect and adoration. In fact,
women were a strong part of the early Celtic Church and many
monasteries had females in positions of authority. For example,
Hilda was Abbess of the double monasteries at Whitby, while
Brigid, who later became St Bride, presided over the monastery
at Kildare.

Pagan to Christian

The transition from paganism to Christianity seems to have been
surprisingly easy. The new religion shared many of the basic
principles of the old. For example, the idea of a father god linked
with that of Dis Pater, Christ with Mabon, the hero-son, and the
concept of the virgin birth resembled the miraculous births of
some of the gods in Celtic myth. Also the Celtic belief in the
spiritual power of the Word was brought to its conclusion in the
opening of St John's Gospel: 'In the beginning was the Word and
the Word was with God and the Word was God.'

In some respects therefore Christianity was presented as the culmination of Druidism. St Columba himself had been trained as a Druid and called Christ his 'drui'. Also by the sixth century, Pope Gregory encouraged the idea of a flow from one religion to the other by suggesting that the old pagan festivals and sites should be retained and sanctified.

Pagan festivals were therefore turned into Christian ones, Yule becoming Christmas and Samhain being replaced with Hallowe'en, which was followed by All Saints Day. Also sacred sites of the old gods were dedicated to the saints. Wells became 'holy wells', while standing stones had crosses carved on them. The names of the gods were also converted into those of the saints. The best example of this is the goddess Brigid who became St Brigid or St Bride and was also identified with the Abbess Brigid. Folk tradition also incorporated her into the nativity story, making her Christ's foster-mother and Mary's midwife.

But some gods were beyond the pale and had to be banished. Cromm Cruaich, the idol who demanded a yearly human sacrifice, was pronounced a demon. A story goes that when St Patrick raised his crozier against him, the idol toppled over and the demon ran shrieking from him.

The veneration of the saints and martyrs led to the cult of relics in which material remains of the body or 'sacred' objects that had been in contact with it were preserved in richly decorated reliquaries, which were enshrined at holy sites and became the object of pilgrimage. Thus the monks achieved sainthood and became the new heroes. Hagiographers wrote tales of their exploits and gave them extraordinary powers reminiscent of those of the Druids. One of the most influential saints was St Columba, also known as Colmcille.

St Columba

Born a prince in Donegal around 521 CE, Columba trained both in the bardic schools and as a monk. He founded the monasteries of Derry, Durrow, probably Kells, and Iona. He was a forceful character. When building Derry he refused to allow the chancel to face east because it would have meant felling a grove of oaks. While at Derry he secretly copied a rare psaltery and then quarrelled with his former tutor, Finnian, over its ownership. The High King of Tara became involved and the situation escalated, ending in a fierce battle on the slopes of Ben Bulben. Three thousand soldiers were killed and, as a penance, Columba took up voluntary exile, on Iona in 563, with twelve companions. His monastery on Iona became one of the most influential foundations. Later the community even accepted some Anglo-Saxons (unlike the Welsh monks, who hated them so much that they refused to evangelize them).

Columba remained in Scotland, mostly on Iona, for the rest of his life except for some important visits to Ireland. In around 580 he attended the assembly of Druim-Cetta at which King Aed mac Ainmirech and other kings attempted to secure the banishment of poets from Ireland. They were becoming too greedy for payment for their poetic services, using the threat of their old powers of satire to make unreasonable demands. But Columba, using his own bardic skills, successfully argued their case and saved them from extinction.

There are several stories of his magical powers. One example was when he outwitted the Druid Briochan by magically making him ill, then curing him with a white stone which he blessed and put into his drink. The saints also had a strong affinity with animals, like that of the old gods and heroes. The story of Columba's mare sensing his approaching death and placing its head on his breast is similar to that of Cu Chulainn's mare crying tears of blood prior to his death. There are numerous stories magically connecting the saints with wild beasts.

The Christianizing of myth

Having no religious ban on the written word – unlike the Druids – the monks painstakingly recorded the gospels. Celtic respect for history prompted them to record the old myths too. While they attempted to Christianize them, they could not disguise their intrinsic character. In some cases, however, a blatant attempt was made to graft new on to old, as in the story of 'The Children of Lir' who were turned into swans for 900 years, long enough for them to survive into the Christian era and encounter St Kernoc, who changed them back into human form. Unhappily they were by then so old that he had to baptize them quickly before they died.

But some of the old heroes were less happily united with the new faith. After Oisin returns from the Land of Youth (see Chapter 7) a further story tells how he was taken to St Patrick to be baptized before dying. In a frank dialogue with St Patrick he argues the cause of the old heroes, especially his father Fionn. When St Patrick tells him that Fionn is in Hell, Oisin retorts: 'Great, then, would be the shame for God not to release Fionn from the shackles of pain; for if God Himself were in bonds my chief would fight on his behalf,' (Hyde) and refuses to be converted.

So, although there were affinities between the two religions, in many ways Christianity must have seemed to the pagan Celts a diminished and less glorious one. Their proud, colourful world-picture in which heroes boasted of their prowess and lived lives of high quest and adventure, was being supplanted by the sombre figures of aesthetic monks. An anonymous sixth-century poem about the coming of St Patrick says:

> *He is coming, Adzed-Head*
> *on the wild-headed sea*
> *with cloak hollow-headed*
> *and curve-headed staff.*
>
> *He will chant false religion*
> *at a bench facing East*
> *and his people will answer*
> *'Amen, amen'*

Kinsella, *New Oxford Book of Verse*

The name given to St Patrick presumably refers to his tonsure.

Despite some scepticism, the pagan Celts were impressed by the monks' harsh life-styles and their powers of endurance on behalf of their faith.

Loricas

The old reverence for the power of verse was carried over into the Celtic Church in the form of Loricas or protective prayers, the most famous being 'St Patrick's Breastplate' or the 'Cry of the Deer':

> *Today I put on*
> *the power of Heaven,*
> *the light of the Sun,*
> *the radiance of the Moon,*
> *the splendour of fire,*
> *the fierceness of lightning*

> Kinsella, *New Oxford Book of Verse*

It was chanted by St Patrick and his monks on an occasion when assassins were lying in wait for them. It magically turned the holy men into the likeness of a herd of deer so that they were able to pass by unhurt.

Celtic Christianity as practised in the monasteries did retain several key features of pagan belief. Their strongest link with the old religion lay in their relationship with nature. In this respect the monastic movement contrasted strongly with Roman Christianity, which was urban in structure, relying on metropolitan sees for its Bishoprics. The Pope even gave a ruling that the office of Bishop could be held only in cities. Because of the lack of towns or cities in Ireland and Wales at this time, it was almost impossible for the Celtic Church to conform to these demands. So, although nominally under the aegis of Rome, the monasteries, particularly those that were especially remote, tended to be autonomous. Nevertheless they followed the strict rules that had first been laid down for them.

Celtic Christianity versus Rome

The first clash between Rome and the Celtic Church came when Pope Gregory sent Augustine to England in 597. He was well received in Kent and became Abbot of Canterbury. He then attempted to make the monasteries acknowledge his papal authority. A meeting was set up between himself and a delegation of seven Celtic bishops. According to Bede the bishops sought a hermit's advice as to whether they should submit to Augustine. The hermit said that if Augustine rose to greet them and treated them with respect then he was a man of God and they should follow him. In the event Augustine did neither, so they refused to submit to his authority.

Thus the Celtic Church continued to follow the old customs. The Synod of Whitby was convened in 664 in an attempt to sort out the differences, which mainly concerned the dating of Easter and the wearing of differing styles of tonsure. The Celtic Church in England reluctantly agreed to conform in these matters, but it caused a split in the community at Lindisfarne, its founder, Bishop Coleman taking his Irish monks back to Iona and leaving it to the English monks. Although agreed in principle, it was many years before the Roman rulings were finally implemented. Wales held out until 1188 with St David's monastery finally complying in 1203 and, in Ireland, groups of monks called Culdees continued to practise Celtic monasticism well into the twelfth century.

Pelagianism

The Church of Rome saw the need to lay down firm doctrines with the result that many of its finest scholars found themselves wrestling with differing ideas. One of these, Pelagius, worried about the doctrine of original sin because it took away the concept of free will and was giving rise to lax morality in Rome. He suggested that man chose to become Christian through free will and was then given God's grace. St Augustine of Hippo argued against him, saying that all partook of original sin with Adam and were bound for Hell unless God chose to save them. The controversy was a heated one and resulted in Augustine's espousing a form of predestination. Eventually the Roman Church accepted the doctrines of Augustine, which carried the implication that original sin was transmitted sexually and that sex was therefore synonymous with sin. One result of this was to reinforce the Roman inclination towards misogyny.

Despite being declared heretical, a modified form of Pelagianism lingered on in the fourth and fifth centuries, particularly in Britain. In holding out against the doctrine of original sin or, at least, its misapplication, Pelagianism seems to reflect the spiritual outlook of the early Celtic Church. For it is noticeable that the exuberance of the poems of the first monks and hermits begins to disappear and their delight in nature and feeling of kinship with God as their 'darling' gradually fades as they take on orthodox Roman thinking.

Thus the elements of pagan belief which had adapted themselves to Christianity, such as reverence for all Creation as expressed in nature and the animal kingdom, respect for matriarchy, an intuitive appreciation of spiritual matters, and a flexibility of belief, became increasingly at variance with the doctrines of the Roman Church. The Celtic Church was unhappy with the urban, hierarchical and patriarchal views of the Romans which came from their pre-Christian philosophical outlook and were at odds with Celtic understanding.

In many ways, therefore, the doctrines of the early saints reflected some of the teachings of the Druids, and it is interesting to note that the Saints and the Druids often exhibited a grudging respect for each other. There is even an account in the 'Life of St Beuno' that on his deathbed he saw a vision of the Holy Trinity together with the Saints *and* the Druids.

Application

Illumination

The monks developed Celtic artistic motifs to a very high and rich level in their illuminated gospels, such as the *Book of Kells*. They recognized the importance of the fusion of artistic with intellectual study. Patterns and symbols can illustrate truths at a deeper level than words on their own. Circles, spirals, the unbroken line and Celtic knotwork were not simply random patterns but significations of spiritual truths. Labyrinths and mazes were religious and, like the sacred wells, consecrated into early Christian use. Walking through a maze allows physical participation in symbolism. Similarly, practising drawing some of the beautiful flowing Celtic designs brings its own rewards and activates the unconscious.

Contemplation of symbolism is also extremely powerful. The Celtic cross is an ancient and all-inclusive symbol. The vertical arm shows the direct line from earth to heaven. The horizontal denotes man's existence on this plane. The point where the two meet is the Omphalos, the still centre. Significantly the Celtic cross incorporates a circle, symbol of wholeness, continuity and completion, as well as representing the feminine. On the Roman cross the circle is missing.

Conclusion

In modern times, Western civilization has developed a materialistic, competitive, male-dominated ethos. It has moved towards a view of the universe in which humanity is alienated from nature and in which the individual sense of community is reduced to an identification with the characters in television soap opera.

These developments have, in part, stemmed from the Industrial Revolution but also from our continued failure to keep pace, spiritually, with our scientific and technological advances. Going back further, it could be argued that our present plight began when the patriarchal rationalism of the Romans superseded the much more balanced and harmonious approach to life followed by the Celts.

This book has described some of the advantages of a Celtic approach to life. These include an awareness of lunar and seasonal cycles, and of humanity's place in nature, and a willingness to acknowledge the power of the unconscious, of emotions, and of the spirit. They also include a recognition of the power of the word, and of symbols as a means of accessing the imagination. Applying these lessons to our lives will have benefits on the individual level, but they are needed even more on the global scale.

At this point in history, human life faces two major threats. The first is our apparent desire – and technical ability – to destroy each other by war. The second is our reckless destruction of the environment. The ancient Celts were not pacifists, but the modern world could certainly learn from their sense of community and equality, and from their regard for truth. We should also learn from, and develop, their sense of the interconnectedness and interdependence of all life forms.

Perhaps above all, we need to learn from the Celtic respect for the feminine, acknowledging that women must be able to play a greater part in world affairs – as for example they have done in the Northern Ireland peace process – in order for the world to survive. On the individual level, we need to cross the bridge between worlds, between the masculine and femine parts of our brain, between conscious and unconscious, in order to become more whole, more creative and less destructive.

Bibliography and Discography

Ammianus Marcellinus (trans. John C. Rolfe), Heinemann, 1950

Caesar (trans. S. A. Handford), *The Conquest of Gaul*, Penguin, 1982

Cross, T. P., and Slover, C. H., *Ancient Irish Tales*, Figgis (Dublin), 1936

Cunliffe, Barry, *The Ancient Celts*, Oxford University Press, 1997

Delaney, Frank, *Legends of the Celts*, Harper-Collins, 1994

Diodorus Siculus (trans. C. H. Oldfather), Historical Library, 1933

Duncan, Anthony, *The Elements of Celtic Christianity*, Element Books, 1992

Ellis, Peter Berresford, *The Druids*, Constable, 1994

— *Caesar's Invasion of Britain*, Constable, 1994

Gantz, Jeffrey (trans.), *The Mabinogion*, Penguin, 1976

Green, Miranda, *Celtic Myths*, British Museum Press, 1993

Hope, Murray, *The Ancient Wisdom of the Celts*, Thorsons, 1995

Hyde, Douglas, *A Literary History of Ireland*, T. Fisher Unwin, 1899

Jackson, Kenneth Hurlstone (trans.), *A Celtic Miscellany*, Penguin, 1971

Joyce, P.W., *Old Celtic Romances*, Longmans, 1920

Jung, Carl, G., *Man and his Symbols*, Penguin 1964

Kinsella, Thomas, *The New Oxford Book of Irish Verse*, OUP, 1992

— (trans.), *The Tain*, OUP, 1990

Laing, Lloyd and Jennifer, *Art of the Celts*, Thames & Hudson, 1992

MacCulloch, J. A., *The Religion of the Ancient Celts*, Constable, 1991

Matthews, Caitlín, *The Celtic Tradition*, Element, 1989

Matthews, Caitlín and John, *The Encyclopaedia of Celtic Wisdom*, Element, 1994

Matthews, John, *Taliesin*, Aquarian Press, 1991
Rolleston, T. W., *Celtic Myths and Legends*, Senate, 1994
Rutherford, Ward, *Celtic Mythology*, Thorsons, 1995
Stewart, R. J., *Celtic Gods Celtic Goddesses*, Blandford, 1997
Strabo (trans. H. L. Jones), *Geography*, Heinemann, 1917
Tacitus (trans. Michael Grant), *The Annals of Imperial Rome*,
    Penguin 1971
Zaczek, Iain, *Chronicles of the Celts*, Collins & Brown, 1996

Music

Noirin Ni Riain, *Celtic Soul*, Earth Music Productions, LMUS 0031
Loreena McKennitt, *Parallel Dreams*, Quinlan Road Ltd, Canada,
    QRCD 103
Celtic Woman (compilation), Celtic Woman Records, CWRCD
    7001
Alan Stivell, *Renaissance of the Celtic Harp*, Rounder Records,
    Massachusetts, CD 3067

Available from C. Hamilton, c/o the publisher, or at:
claire@hamiltonharps.freeserve.co.uk
Company of Strangers, *Blodeuwedd – A Wife out of Flowers*, COS 298
— *The Love-Song of Diarmid and Grainne*, CSSM1 (cassette)
The Celtic Harp, Sound and Media Ltd, SUMCD 4133
Celtic Harp Moods, Carlton Home Entertainment Ltd, 30 360 00822

Index

Aenghus Mac Og 24, 25
air, element 9–10, 15
Amergin 31, 71–2
anima-animus 57–8
Arawn 52–3
Arianrhod 26, 33–4, 41, 74
art, Celtic 19, 20, 39, 86
astrology 20, 50
Augustine, St 84
Augustine of Hippo, St 84

bards 61–2
bean-sidhe 54, 57
Beltain 48–49, 50
Blodeuwedd 26, 34, 40–2
Boann 10, 24, 25
boasting 71, 73
Boudicca 8, 30, 76
Boyne, River 10, 24
Bran 27, 54
Brehons 63–5, 75
Bricriu 32
Brigid 14, 23, 48, 79, 80
Brythonic 4
Buddhism 38, 57
burials 19, 57

Caesar, Julius 5, 18
Calatin, daughters of 35
cauldron
    Ceridwen's 12, 22, 43
    Dagda's 15
    grail derived from 44
    Gundestrup 11, 15, 24, 58
Celts
    appearance 6
    characters 5, 29–30
    origin of name 1
    origins of people 3–4
    territories 4
Ceridwen 12, 22, 42–3
Cernunnos 24
Christianity
    Britain, arrival in 78
    monasticism 25, 75, 83–4
    paganism, and 23, 48, 79–81, 85
Coligny calendar 46–7, 50, 62
Columba, St 80–1
Conan 74
Conchobar 34
Connal Cernach 32
Conle 54
constellations 9

Cormac mac Art 53
Corpry 62
Cross, symbol 10, 14, *86*
Culwch and Olwen 34
Cu Chulainn 8, 16, 21, 22, 25, 31–6, 56, 71
curses 33–4, 41–2, 65

Dagda 15, 24, 25, 55
Danu 21, 23
Dechtire 34
Delphi, sack of 4
Dindsenchas 15–16, 61, 71
democracy 76
Directions, Four 13
Dis Pater 23, 46, 79
divination 38, 61, 62, 65, 68–9
dreams 19, 61
Druids 9, 14, 15, 60–9

earth, element 9, 13, 14
elements 9–12, 13, *45*
Emer 16, 35, 56
Epona 16, 22
Eriu 20
Etain 25, 53
Etarcomol 31–2

Fann 35, 56
Fergus mac Roth 34
festivals 47–50, 51
Fianna 49, 73
Finegas 31, 73
Fionn mac Cumhail 7, 31, 32–3, 58, 73
Firbolgs 7
fire, element 10, 13, 14
Fomorians 7, 24, 25
Friuch and Rucht 40

geasa 32–3, 36
Glastonbury 9
gods
    dark 21–2
    depictions of 19, 20
    land, and 19
    naming 18, 19
    Roman 18, 19, 23, 25
Goidelic 4
Grainne 25, 32–3
Gwion Bach 12
Gwydion 26, 33, 40–2, 72, 74

Hallowe'en 27, 48
Hallstatt culture 3
head, cult of 27

healing 11, 14, 23, 62
hero 29, 31–2, 36–7
honour 32, 73–4
horses 8, 16, 22–3, 49, 81

Imbolc 23, 48
immrama 53–4
Invasions, Book of 7
Irish Republicanism 13, 36

justice 74–6

Labraid 56
language groups 4
Laoghaire 32
La Tène culture 3, 11
laws 63–5, 75
Liban 56
Lindow Man 12, 67
Lir, children of 26, 82
Lleu Llaw Gyffes 25, 33–4, 41–2, 74
Loeg 34–5
Loegaire mac Crimthann 53
loricas 83
Lugaid 35, 36
Lugh 14, 25, 49, 65
lunar calendar 46–7, 50
Lughnasadh 49–50

Mabinogion 7, 21
Mabon 10, 25, 79
Maelduin 54
Macha 23, 35, 49–50
Manannan mac Lir 10, 26, 54, 58
Math Mathonwy 26, 34, 40–2
matriarchy 6, 20, 24
Medb 8, 9, 32, 35
Mercury 25, 49
Midhir 25, 53
Milesians 7
Minerva 23
mistletoe 9, 66
Mongan, King 58
moon 46–7, 51
Morgan Le Fay 21
Morrigan 21–2, 24, 35, 39
mother goddesses 8, 9, 20, 23
Moytura, battle of 7, 24, 65
music 2, 31, 55, 61
mythical sources 6–7

naming 71
nature, reverence for 8, 19, 79, 85, 87
Nechtan 10, 25
Newgrange 9, 25
Niamh 35
Nuada 25

oak 66
Ogham alphabet 26, 31, 33, 50, 62–3, 64, 68–9
Oghma 26
Oisin 53, 82
omens 35–6
oral tradition 1–2, 5
Otherworld 9, 18, 38, 52–5
ovates 62

Patrick, St 80, 82
Pelagianism 84–5
place, sense of 15–16, 71
poetry 23, 39, 42, 62, 71–3, 77, 81
Provinces of Ireland, Five 13
Pwll 52–3
Pythagoras 58

reincarnation 57–8
Rhiannon 22–3, 53, 74
river names 16
Romans 3, 4, 30, 67
Rome, sack of 3

Sabrann 10
sacrifice 12, 26, 29, 66–7
Salmon of Knowledge 31
Samhain 27, 31, 45, 48
satire 62, 72
Scathach 21, 31
Sencha 31
Senchan Torpeist 72–3
shape-shifting 12, 21, 26, 39–41
soul loss 57–8
Spear of Lugh 7, 14
Stone of Destiny 7, 14
Sulis 10
sun 10, 46, 50
Sword of Nuada 7, 15

Tain Bo Cuailnge 7
Taliesin 12, 42–4, 73
Tara 9, 14, 48
time 45, 55
totemism 20, 22, 24, 39, 62
triple-aspecting 20, 21–2, 23, 48, 79
truth, power of 70, 77
Tuan mac Caraill 7, 40
Tuatha de Danann 7, 9, 15, 19, 21, 25, 53

Underworld 9, 19, 24, 53
Urnfield culture 3

water 3, 10–12, 13, 15, 53
wells 10–11, 23, 80
Whitby, Synod of 84
women, position of 6, 63, 76, 79, 88
writing, Celts' avoidance of 1–2, 5, 50, 70